COURAGEOUSLY
SOFT

COURAGEOUSLY SOFT

DARING TO KEEP A TENDER
HEART IN A TOUGH WORLD

CHARAIA RUSH

BakerBooks

a division of Baker Publishing Group
Grand Rapids, Michigan

Published by Baker Books
a division of Baker Publishing Group
Grand Rapids, Michigan
BakerBooks.com

Printed in the United States of America

Library of Congress Cataloging-in-Publication Data
Names: Rush, Charaia, 1991– author.
Title: Courageously soft : daring to keep a tender heart in a tough world / Charaia Rush.
Description: Grand Rapids, Michigan : Baker Books, a division of Baker Publishing Group, [2024] | Includes bibliographical references.
Identifiers: LCCN 2023032419 | ISBN 9781540903433 (paper) | ISBN 9781540903860 (cloth) | ISBN 9781493444083 (ebook)
Subjects: LCSH: Spiritual healing. | Healing—Religious aspects—Christianity.
Classification: LCC BT732.5 .R78 2024 | DDC 234/.131—dc23/eng/20230927
LC record available at https://lccn.loc.gov/2023032419

The author is represented by Alive Literary Agency, www.AliveLiterary.com.

Baker Publishing Group publications use paper produced from sustainable forestry practices and post-consumer waste whenever possible.

24   25   26   27   28   29   30   7   6   5   4   3   2   1

To the ones who believe
your soft heart is a curse,
may this book be a benediction
over your sacred tenderness.

CONTENTS

INTRODUCTION

Soft Heart and Tough Feet

Growing up, I lost count of the number of times my mother sat me down and explained the need to toughen up. Hard days at school were followed by meetings with my mother in our kitchen, her finger positioned under my chin as she whispered, "You're too soft, baby girl." The phrase rang in my ears like a song I had to sing to get out of my head. And so I whispered the words aloud until the rhythm conceived a new truth: soft hearts aren't meant to survive. And I wanted to be a survivor.

We enter this world with a heart that's hard by nature, resistant to the pliable posture that hearts held by the King require. We say yes to life with God and are given the gift of a new heart. And then life does what life is known to do—introduce pain, disappointment, and despair to any slight tenderness. This perpetual hardening of the human heart is a gradual transformation. A slow turn in the shadow of our souls. A shift that generally goes unnoticed.

Until we do notice.

Until we struggle to extend compassion, to not see with a gaze hazed by cynicism, to believe God is who He says He is and not what our bitterness portrays Him to be. There is a tension that exists as our beings tread this space between the garden and glory. And though the journey doesn't lead to an easing of the strain that comes from living in the space between now and eternity, we survive by keeping soft hearts in the shell of our humanity.

And the keeping is a fight.

It's a fight we wage in the dark, in the storm, and in the desert. It's a resolve to contend to believe that every day presents an opportunity to "see the goodness of the LORD in the land of the living" (Ps. 27:13 NIV). It's the discipline of extending compassion when we are inclined to merely extend distanced commentary, keeping ourselves out of the fray. Staying soft is the fruit of the courageous fights we wage in the seasons of our suffering and the moments of our indignation.

The life of Jackie Pullinger illustrates this fight for a tender heart. Pullinger is what I would consider a silent saint. At age twenty-two, in 1966, she boarded the cheapest ship she could find that was traveling port to port and waited for God to tell her where to disembark. After more than a dozen stops, she arrived in Hong Kong. She found herself in what was called the Walled City, a small, overly populated, and lawless area filled with refugees who had fled to Hong Kong as the Cultural Revolution began in China. For almost a half century, Pullinger dedicated her life to working with those being exploited in sex work, gang members, and those "chasing the dragon"—a term to describe young Hong Kong men in crazed pursuit of opioids.

In her autobiography, Pullinger describes how as followers of Jesus our actions and our hearts must come under His submission as we carry the gospel to those who are desperate for hope. "God wants us to have soft hearts and hard feet. The trouble with so many of us is that we have hard hearts and soft feet."[1] In a 2020 interview with the nonprofit organization Alpha, when asked what a soft heart is, Pullinger states that though she doesn't know how to explain it, she believes a heart must break in order to stay softened. She then explains that her understanding of what the Son of God did for her is what enables her to couple her soft heart with the hard feet needed to go and love those around her.[2]

The balance of a soft heart paired with tough feet is a beautiful illustration of the gospel we carry in our frail humanity. And yet we constantly find ourselves tempted to trade. Tragedy, unspoken disappointments, harbored offenses, unhealed trauma—they all show up on our porches like a door-to-door salesperson, petitioning us to exchange our tenderness for a toughness that promises to keep us safe. They offer us a pitch that we are safer within the confines of the hardened walls of our hearts.

And yet, this posture, this hardened state of the heart, contradicts the Savior's desire for us. In Mark 3, Jesus enters the synagogue on the Sabbath and sees a man with a withered hand. The scene is set up perfectly to display the miraculous work of Christ and entice wonder among those who witness it. Instead, the religious leaders watch Jesus not with a desire to be thrilled by seeing the Son of Man restoring what would remain broken without His touch but with contempt. Their eyes are filled with cynicism, and their hearts are callous from their rigid devotion to the law. When they question Jesus for healing a man on the Sabbath, He confronts them by asking if they were so blinded by their devotion to the law that they could not see the foolishness of protesting the good work of healing on the Sabbath. The crowd falls silent, and Jesus looks at them "with anger, grieved at their hardness of heart" (Mark 3:5 ESV).

Christ's response to the hearts of the religious leaders in the synagogue that day is a mix of righteous indignation and holy grief at the evidence of their hardened hearts. A hard heart isn't just carried in the shadows unheard—it has a voice, and it whispers over the character of God. It looks to accuse His goodness, it fails to extend compassion toward those with withered hands, and it's unmoved by the presence of God. As Charles Spurgeon says, "hardening is of the worst kind when it takes place in the heart."[3]

The Good News of the gospel is not simply that Jesus came, walked among us, and took on our sin for our salvation. The whole gospel runs deep with our simultaneously instant and continuous transformation—in Christ the old is made new, the dead are made alive, and hearts of stone are replaced with hearts of flesh. He promises, "I will remove the heart of stone from their flesh and give them a heart of flesh" (Ezek. 11:19 ESV). His resurrecting power forms the impossible: flesh from our stony hearts.

This promise of resurrection is a phenomenon requiring divine power that only comes from His sovereign grace. You cannot persuade a rock to become flesh, nor offer it enough promises to get it to produce something it's incapable of producing. As Charles Spurgeon writes,

Every grace leans towards tenderness, and the whole current of the divine life sets that way. You cannot be strong in piety unless you are tender in heart. . . . There must be tenderness. It is an essential point. Unless it is melted down the hard metal cannot be poured into the mould and fashioned for use and beauty. The Lord Jesus will never set his seal upon cold wax, he stamps his image on hearts of flesh and not on stones.[4]

This is what I know: staying soft isn't the fruit of our might but the fullness of a miracle. The miracle of our humanity being held by His divinity. The miracle of remaining radically devoted to hope—humming its melody even as we tread through the valley of the shadow of death. The miracle of a heart of stone that starts to beat again with the life of resurrection.

Whenever we examine our hearts and find them still tender, we can be moved with gratitude, as this is evidence of divine power at work within us. For our hope is found in the truth that the Spirit of God pursues us in our ruined nature. He who made us can make us new again and again.

The promise spoken by the prophet Ezekiel is as true today as when it was written. He melts our hearts of steel. He can change a "hard as a lower millstone" heart (Job 41:24) into flesh courageous enough to feel. There's no heart too hard when touched by His hand.

Toni Morrison once said, "If you find a book you really want to read but it hasn't been written yet, then you must write it."[5] This book is the letter I wish I had found on the shores of my own seasons of deep sorrow and suffering. It's the words I wish I'd read when I was tempted to trade my tender heart for something armored—and when I did just that.

This book is for those, like me, contending to believe that staying soft isn't just the better way but the braver way. I pray this book is a soft place to land. A holy space to believe again in the power of the Spirit of God at work in and through us. I pray He honors every tear these pages catch and solidifies every word you mark with a crooked line and your favorite pen. I pray this book gets passed along and never returned because it's passed along again.

It's costly to be courageously soft. My mother's plea for me to "toughen" up was her attempt to protect me from a world that had only proven to dismiss and destroy softness. It's scary to consider what it might look like to live with our hearts tender after being beaten down.

But this tough world needs tender hearts. And the moment we lean into the perceived weakness of staying soft is the moment we walk in the power of being pliable. The hands of God long to heal the hurt in this world by molding our tenderness into tangible evidence that His goodness is still at play.

> Hearts of stone, relent relent!
> Break, by Jesus' cross subdued.[6]

1

THE STORIES WE LET OUR WOUNDS WRITE

*Discovering the Origin Story
of Your Hardened Heart*

It was late summer. A year earlier, I'd made the gut-wrenching decision to reconcile with my husband after he had repeatedly violated our vows. It felt like the right thing to do. I'd moved back to Colorado for a time, but returning to my husband felt like I'd put on an honorable superhero suit— the godly wife who fought for her marriage and defeated all odds. But one night in July I discovered that the season of reconciliation I believed we were in was an illusion.

In a matter of days, my life flipped upside down. I packed my books, the kids' toys, and the fragments of my life, and began the move home to Colorado. Again. And my story of redemption became a cluttered mess of failure. I spent many nights lying on an air mattress in my grandmother's basement, my mind filled with questions haunting me with the reality of the devastation of my situation.

Why is this happening to me?
Why did my spouse betray me?
Why wasn't I enough?
Why couldn't my marriage be fixed?

Night after night, the questions began to calcify lies into "truth." I went from asking "Why did God allow this to happen?" to stating "God didn't protect me because He doesn't care." Losing my marriage was the worst-case scenario, and I decided that if I was going to survive, I needed to armor up, even against God, who I perceived did not and would not protect me. Feeling that sense of power to protect myself made me feel like I had some control in a situation that was spiraling out of my grasp.

Years earlier, when I was pregnant and first found out I was having a boy, I knew my world would become filled with superheroes and action figures. I was never interested in the web of the Marvel universe until I realized a basic understanding of it was one way to connect with my son. After several movie nights, I found myself watching these movies and becoming completely immersed in the origin stories.

In the 2007 film *Spider-Man 3*, the final installment of the series starring Tobey Maguire, the plot begins a year after the hero's nemesis, Doc Oc, sacrifices himself. Peter Parker's relationship with Mary Jane is finally in a good place, and Mary Jane lands her first role on Broadway. On the night Peter is set to propose, a meteorite lands near the two, and an extraterrestrial symbiote follows Peter to his apartment. It's not long before Peter Parker (Spider-Man) discovers new information about the killing of his uncle. Peter is tormented by nightmares of his uncle's murder, and when he learns that the Sandman—a shapeshifter he sees as a villain—was personally involved, this discovery unleashes new reserves of rage in Peter.

The symbiote, an alien organism, is attracted to Peter's growing rage and attaches itself to his body, ultimately transforming his suit into a black one. Peter's first reaction to his new suit is one of excitement and pleasure, as it enhances his powers and makes him feel more powerful. However, as the story progresses, he realizes that the symbiote is also affecting his behavior and causing him to be more and more aggressive and selfish. The black suit is undeniably powerful, but its power seems to be derived of vengeance. This creates conflict between Peter and everyone around him, including Mary Jane and his best friend, Harry.

The turning point in the story comes when Peter chooses to remove the symbiote, a symbolic act of shedding his negative impulses and embracing his true heroic nature. He then faces his guilt and forgives his uncle's killer, a transformative experience that allows him to become a better version of himself and a more noble Spider-Man. And the black suit seeks out a new host.

For Peter Parker and for all of us, *every origin story of a hardened heart points back to a wound.* The backstory of a tough heart almost always carries a storyline filled with scars. The armor we create for ourselves seems to make us stronger. Just like Spider-Man experienced a new level of power and heightened ability when he operated with the black symbiote, it can feel good to feel powerful, especially after we've been so hurt. But the truth is, the armor is an illusion of protection that only keeps us from healing.

The black suits we clothe ourselves with are the stories we let our wounds write. It's this act of armoring ourselves that allows our disappointment to interpret the promises of God. We let rejection tell us about our worth. We let our pain tell us about the character of God. We let our trauma tell us about hope. When we tell ourselves the story that God isn't who He says He is and that our hearts are not safe in His hand, we'll find our reflections about Him look more like our pain in the mirror than His good character.

Our True Origin Story

"Both the man and his wife were naked, yet felt no shame," the first book in the Bible tells us (Gen. 2:25). But what might have been a romantic opener to God's story with humankind in Genesis takes a quick turn. God makes the world and everything in it, creates man and woman in the perfect garden—and before you know it, they're kicked out, dealing with fear, shame, and a feeling of disconnection from God. I don't pretend to understand how this story is supposed to encourage us, but what I do know is that God's constant desire to redeem humanity is always the center of the story.

In the beginning, Adam and Eve live in the complete absence of sin. They are free to be naked without shame because they're clothed with the garments of being fully seen and loved by God. But sin enters the world with their choice. When the woman believes the cunning serpent and grabs the forbidden fruit. When the man believes the word of his wife over the Word of the Lord. When they pierce the fruit's flesh with their teeth, believing that what the serpent promised would outshine God's glorious promise if they obey Him. And in Genesis 3:7 we see the chaotic turn of events: "Then the eyes of both of them were opened, and they knew they were naked; so they sewed fig leaves together and made coverings for themselves."

Their eyes are opened. And in that moment they try to cover themselves with suits crafted with their own hands. Their fig leaves become their armor. Shame interrupts their communion with God, and the bodies that were once safe to live bare and exposed are now in need of covering. When sin enters, the story changes, and humankind begins to hide and resist the very hands that formed their being.

We live through many moments of our eyes being opened. Moments where we respond to the brokenness of this world by frantically gathering fig leaves to protect our bareness. Our shame and fear drive the need to cover up, and we layer on the leaves of cynicism, self-righteousness, bitterness, and unforgiveness. We believe we are saving ourselves by hiding from God. We believe we are safe by running from the haven found in trusting God with our pain, which would require us to be too vulnerable and too exposed.

Free will is a tricky gift God gives. We are free to choose. The origin story in Genesis is marked by humanity's choices—which are often painful and hard—but as we continue in the stories of the Bible, we learn that the pain can be redeemed by Christ's choices. Heroes have this in common just as much as villains: *their storylines begin with a wound.* And by the wounds of Christ, the deepest wounds of our origin stories are healed. By His wounds the script is changed and we are granted the gift of salvation. And the miracle of salvation is that, by the Spirit of the living God, we get a new birth story—the miracle of our origins made new.

Ezekiel 11 encourages the Israelites in exile with a promise of restoration that would be fulfilled through Christ. The Lord, speaking through the prophet, makes it clear that our origin story is meant to be rewritten through the restoration of our hearts: "I will give them integrity of heart and put a new spirit within them; I will remove their heart of stone from their bodies and give them a heart of flesh" (Ezek. 11:19).

The new covenant established on the cross begins a new origin story, one that centers on the wounds Jesus sustained so that we are not bound by a story that reduces us to our scars. But even with a new story, receiving the miracle of our hearts becoming flesh and returning to tenderness depends upon our choice. We cannot be made soft unless we dare to contend for tenderness through our surrender, and that surrender is our choice alone.

Do Not Harden Your Heart

Psalm 95 speaks of how God is worthy of our humble worship and how we were created to proclaim His greatness by joyfully singing His praise. But amid this commandment to do what we were made to do, there is a warning against doing what we tend to do.

> Today, if only you would hear his voice,
> *"Do not harden your hearts as you did at Meribah."*
> (Ps. 95:7–8 NIV)

In order to understand this reference to Meribah, we must go back to Exodus. The Israelites have been miraculously rescued from the grip of Pharaoh. They are free and on their way to the land God has promised them. A land on the other side of a wilderness where the Israelites would find themselves wandering for forty years because of their own rebellion.

The Israelites witnessed the hand of God on Egypt turning water into crimson blood, covering the skies with insects, and finally striking down the firstborn of all who did not fear His name. They witnessed the wonder of waters being parted to make a pathway through the middle of the Red Sea. Walking through walls of water on either side, they moved, I'm sure, with both fear they would be captured again and in awe of God's deliverance.

But what they witnessed to be true of God does not sustain them for long in the desert. One minute they're receiving the answer to their pleas, and the next minute they're begging to return to Egypt because they don't trust God to provide water in the middle of the desert (Num. 20:1–3). And though we are tempted to look at the Israelites and scoff at their disobedience and rebellion, their actions are not surprising. The Israelites are living with the trauma of being enslaved through four generations. According to Exodus 1:14, the Egyptians had been ruthless in their oppression and made the Israelites' lives bitter. When Moses first told the Israelites God's plan to free them, "they did not listen to him because of their broken spirit" (6:9). Freedom away from Egypt does not change the Israelites' origin story, which is filled with pain, misery, oppression, and what feels like years of silence from the Lord. The desert is the place of redemption. A wilderness that presents a choice to trust God to make tender what years of enslavement have made tough.

And Meribah is the place where God's people choose to harden their hearts.

The psalmist does not say "do not *let* your hearts grow hard" or "fight against the ways this world will *make* your heart hard." Rather, the call is to not harden your *own* heart, demonstrating the personal responsibility and agency of choice alive in all of us. This call makes plain what is evident all through the Scripture: we harden our own hearts.

And why wouldn't we? Life is unbearable at times—we suffer hardship and disappointment, failure and tragedy. The news is full of crisis after crisis. It's easy to harden our hearts. Still, the pattern of Scripture is that time and time again, we see God confronting this human inclination to rebel and grow hard. To lean into the lies of the serpent tangled on the branches of the tree. To bear witness to the miracles of His hand and then, in the very next moment, to allow our forgetfulness to inform our faith.

> We harden our hearts when we pretend to be what we are not: gods ourselves.
>
> We harden our hearts when we make an idol of what we can do for God.
>
> We harden our hearts when we withhold forgiveness because we've distanced ourselves from the mercy that greets us each and every day.
>
> We harden our hearts when we dethrone God as Lord and seat our own appetites for vengeance and control in His place.

We aren't to blame for the wounds that are inflicted on our hearts. Becoming soft is not denying that life hurts our hearts in ways we could never imagine. But our response to what we experience, to the collateral damage of living in a broken world and opening our hearts to broken people, is ours alone to decide.

The author of Hebrews writes repeatedly about the importance of resisting the very real tendency to let unbelief harden us. Quoting from Psalm 95 and recalling the same incident at Meribah, the writer shows how the path of a hardened heart is one of rebellion. It's a deceitful path, as it has us pursuing something we can never receive without surrendering our armor: a life of wholeness and true freedom. But every hardened heart stems from the same origin story: pain and choice.

> See to it, brothers and sisters, that none of you has a sinful, unbelieving heart that turns away from the living God. But encourage one another daily, as long as it is called "Today," so that none of you may be hardened by sin's deceitfulness. We have come to share in Christ, if indeed we hold our original conviction firmly to the very end.
>
> As has just been said:
>
> "Today, if you hear his voice,
>   *do not harden your hearts*
>   *as you did in the rebellion."* (Heb. 3:12–15 NIV)

Unbelief lives underneath the surface of our hardened hearts. This truth hearkens back to the moment in the garden when Eve let the serpent plant a seed of unbelief: "Did God really say . . . ?" (Gen. 3:1). When recalling God's command,

Eve shows that, in her heart, she does not believe in the fullness of what God had spoken. And this same disbelief sits in the hearts of the Israelites—who know what God had said but don't believe He meant it.

There was a choice made in the garden.

There was a choice to be made on the cross.

There is a choice to be made regarding our hearts.

When we are in the middle of our own wilderness, pained with hunger and tempted to think that God led us there to leave us there, we must decide not to harden our own hearts. When we are in lush pastures and are tempted to believe that what we craft with our own hands is better than the best God wants to give us through our obedience, we must decide not to harden our own hearts. When we are disappointed and betrayed and tempted to allow our wounds to become weapons, we must decide not to harden our own hearts.

The Miracle of Soft

A hardened heart isn't a happenstance. The truth is that staying soft is a courageous decision. With fear and trembling, we welcome God's tenderness and transformation even when we want to protect our hearts our own way.

You've already heard me refer to this transformation of the heart as a *miracle*, and I can't say that enough. So it's important that I define what it means and why I believe a soft heart to be miraculous work. The preservation of our softness by the Spirit of God points to His glory and to a hope that our origin stories have been redeemed and restored through

Christ. Precisely because it is so unlikely, so outlandish, and so against the grain, the miracle of a soft heart authenticates the message of the gospel. It carries the good news that not only are we not left to the natural state of our hearts but we can always return to softness when we settle back into His sovereign hand to be shaped and formed anew. It's the kind of miracle that ignites a sense of wonder within those around us as they witness the kindness of God in contrast to the cruelty of this world. And God invites us to partake in this miracle: "Today, if you hear [My] voice, do not harden your hearts" (Heb. 3:15).

Pain has two paths, resentfulness or redemption. I am not naive to how challenging it is to welcome God's presence into your life and relationships. I'm in this struggle with you, and I have walked both paths. What I know now is that one path tends to produce more fear and the other more faith. My invitation to you is not that you will never experience pain, doubt, or fear but that you realize keeping a soft heart through it all is essential to redeeming it.

My prayer for you is that you choose *soft*. That you allow the Holy Spirit to massage the hardened bits of your heart back into tender flesh that beats alive as it was always meant to. That you might trust God's protection and power in your pain. That you'd hold on for a miracle in your soul.

I pray you will hear His voice within these pages. I pray that your belief will be resurrected. I pray your eyes will be opened to the powerful miracle that is staying soft in a hard world.

2

MIRAGES AND MARA MOMENTS

*Naming Your Pain While Refusing
to Let Your Pain Name You*

The best advice I was given about writing was to commit to telling the truth. Ernest Hemingway said, "A writer should be of as great probity and honesty as a priest of God. He is either honest or not."[1] Ordination into the "priesthood" of being a writer is for those who do not forfeit their truth-telling for storytelling but instead tell the story of life with the truth of being human.

This is my truth: I've written portions of this book with a heart that was anything but soft. I stared at the screen waiting for words that I needed for my own journey. I struggled with softness and wrestled with the daunting feeling that this work was making a mockery of my life. I faced questions that

forced me to dig deeper into softness as more than a senti-
mental concept. *How am I supposed to be the spokesperson for
softness when my own suffering is having its way with my heart?*

I need you to know that I am not writing from the high
place of having arrived but as someone in the trenches contending to be brave enough to stay soft, just like you.

When you hear "stay soft," you may be prone to believe
you can achieve tenderness by playing dress-up. You drape
yourself with the layers of the things you should be saying,
the ways you should be acting, and what you should believe
to be true. It's normal for your first reaction to be the act of
covering yourself with the shadow of softness, desperately
attempting to find refuge by pretending the world hasn't had
its way with your heart. But you cannot break the concrete
case around your heart by impersonating the fruit of a soft
heart. You cannot arrive at tenderness by avoiding honesty.

My grandparents lived in Arizona for most of my childhood. We didn't visit them frequently, but when we did my
dad would drive us from Colorado, because flying as a family
of four wasn't economical. Somehow we always found ourselves in the hellish climate of Arizona right in the middle
of summer. The week would be spent inside of my grandparents' home staring out the window at the pavement we
were forbidden to walk on, as we hid from the sun we were
told would scorch our ebony skin.

It was miserable.

Despite the boring week inside that pink stucco house,
I did enjoy the journey there. I would lean my head against
the car window and watch the warped mirages float above

the highway. I knew we were on land. I felt the bumps of the potholes as our tires dipped into each one, and my stomach did somersaults from the car sickness that would only subside with a cracked window. But no matter what I knew to be true, the more I gazed through the glass, the more my mind convinced me that I was witnessing a river instead of a solid road.

Living softly isn't living fixated on a mirage of how we wish life to be. For years I upheld the illusion of reconciliation in my marriage. I believed that remaining tender could only happen if I pretended as though the smoke I was smelling wasn't coming from *inside* the house. And, as John Mayer sings, I was "slow dancing in a burning room,"[2] desperate to extinguish the flames with my denial. I began calling my delusion "hope" to avoid the inevitable. And I believed I could manufacture the miracle of staying soft by grasping at what I wished would be instead of grappling with the reality of what was.

The thing about illusions is that the layers of the mirage disappear as we get closer. *The distance keeps the illusion alive.* I think back to the times I would pretend I was soft. The times I burrowed myself in what was expected of me in order to uphold the illusions of peace and comfort I longed for. We tend to keep these illusions alive by keeping God at a distance with our Christian platitudes. We only touch Him with a ten-foot pole—while bandaging ourselves with counterfeit hope that refuses to reckon with reality. In doing so, we dodge Christ, who is the substance and sustainer of hope, and instead seek quick relief by saying all the right things.

In Joan Didion's book *The White Album*, she writes, "we tell ourselves stories in order to live."[3] Sometimes we tell ourselves stories filled with half-truths to live in seasons we refuse to be honest about. And there is a sense of comfort when we project an illusion onto the landscape of our lives. We are convinced we are being made soft by sticking to a story filled with denial of our pain, despair, and disappointment. Perhaps this is because honesty brings its own ache; it requires us to face the things we want to avoid. But a life filled with mirages that satisfy what we wish was our reality strips us of the power that lies in testifying to what is.

Your wounds can make such illusions attractive. And you may be tempted to dive into this book with a resolve to continue pretending. To flip through the pages dedicated to only let the Spirit of God skim over the surface of your heart. Giving Him room to make you soft enough to keep up appearances but never receiving the tenderness that comes from telling the truth at the feet of Jesus.

I want you to receive the softening that comes from being bravely honest in the secret place with the King of your heart. Being honest about the pain isn't just saying "it hurt" but making plain the beliefs that have bubbled up from your scars.

There is a transformation that happens when we stop trying to "achieve" softness and instead accept the work of being made tender by naming our pain. And in doing so, when we allow ourselves to be held by God as we are honest about our hurt, we resist the threat of becoming hard by being named by our pain. The truth is, if we don't name our pain honestly and openly, it will end up naming us.

Our Mara Moments

I had been in labor for eight hours. I was finally able to remove the mask that was making breathing difficult—the byproduct of birthing in the middle of a pandemic. My phone, propped on a tripod, held my husband's face as he watched from the other side of the world due to his deployment. My doula, whom I had met a month prior, held my hand while I worked my way through the contractions that grew closer and harsher. Suddenly I broke down and, with a heavy breath, released the words "I can't do this." My doctor looked at me with eyes both gentle and strong, and my doula pulled me into her chest.

It was as if each woman in the room knew that my proclamation of defeat was about more than this moment and had been given a preview into my journey up until that point. A journey that started when my husband left for seven months to join the military, only to confess after his return that he had been unfaithful during his time away. A journey that was filled with me uttering "It's ok, I forgive you"—a knee-jerk reaction to desperately save my marriage because divorce was never an option. It's like they knew each tear they were witnessing carried a scene from this season. Clips of me solo parenting while pregnant in the middle of a pandemic with my spouse deployed. Enduring sleepless nights after hearing my spouse tell me he didn't love me anymore. Rubbing my belly, confident that the baby I was carrying would bring my husband back to me.

They knew none of this, but they held me like they did. They covered me when we all glanced at my phone and witnessed my husband sleeping. They smiled weakly when I shouted, "I love you!" to him through the tears as I held our daughter—and was met with silence before he muttered he was tired and the call ended.

As grateful as I was to have been so well cared for, life had already done its work on me, and the day my daughter was born was also the day my soft heart ceased to be. I had chosen the mirage for too long, living in denial and only seeing what I wanted to see. But no more. In that moment I felt like Naomi, whispering to those who looked at the shambles of my life, "I'm not who I was. Life has had its way with me. Don't call me Charaia, call me by my pain." It was my Mara moment, and I chose to be marked by my despair.

The book of Ruth begins by introducing us to Naomi. Her husband, Elimelech, takes her and their two sons out of Bethlehem and toward Moab. They leave the promised land of Israel to head back into the wilderness from which they'd been delivered. After they arrive, both sons marry, but then Elimelech and his two sons die, leaving Naomi in the most disadvantaged class in the ancient world: a childless widow with no man to claim her as his own daughter or wife or mother.

Desperate for redemption in a very bleak situation, Naomi plans to return to Bethlehem, for she "heard in Moab that the LORD had come to the aid of his people by providing food for them" (Ruth 1:6 NIV). Even in this tragic situation, she knows there is no hope found by moving farther away from God. The story continues with Ruth, one of her daughters-in-law, proclaiming her loyalty and accompanying Naomi back to her homeland.

Naomi and Ruth's trek back to Bethlehem is extremely dangerous. They likely are traveling during the late summer, through the Judean wilderness near the Dead Sea. Aside from the environmental threats, this is not a safe journey for two women alone. And yet, the knowledge that she's heading toward the very thing she needs makes Naomi both willing and brave.

When they enter Bethlehem, "the whole town was excited about their arrival" (v. 19). Naomi is known among her people, and her arrival brings excitement. Perhaps it's because they know Bethlehem is where she belongs or are relieved to see that living in the land of their enemies hasn't taken their friend's life. But soon their initial joy is hushed as they ask one another, "Can this be Naomi?" It is as though the lines on her face carry the story of the last ten years—aged by time and worn out by grief. Her skin holds the scenes where she lost her husband and two sons. Naomi's pain spills out of her being. So it's no surprise she responds this way:

> "*Don't call me Naomi. Call me Mara*," she answered, "for the Almighty has made me very bitter. I went away full, but the Lord has brought me back empty. Why do you call me Naomi, since the Lord has opposed me, and the Almighty has afflicted me?" (vv. 20–21)

Naomi's confession—her Mara moment—represents a crossroads and a choice made between three paths in response to her suffering. One path can only be walked if Naomi believes her identity is wrapped in her pain. The second path is one of following the mirages on the road of denial. Finally, the last path is filled with rock and gravel that whisper for her to offer up the truth of her pain with hope that God can enter it.

We all face such a crossroads in our pain. We can deny the pain altogether, let our pain name us and overshadow our true identity, or openly cry out and name our pain to God and let Him hold us. While denial may promise to smooth out the sharp edges of our hearts after breaking, and while settling into our own Mara moment might feel validating for a time, neither of these choices make room for God to enter our personal psalms of honesty.

Ultimately, God with us in our pain is the only thing that can stop the turning of our hearts toward the hard places. When we allow ourselves to be held in our pain, we are free to speak the truth and also wrestle against the urges to deny our pain or claim it as our identity. In Christ we endure pain tethered to the promise that we are not defined by it. We can name what has happened to us honestly and remain free from bondage to our pain.

See, Naomi wants to be called a different name. Nestled under her confession is a belief that the sum of her identity is her affliction. But the author of Ruth refuses to accommodate such a lie. We don't see the author suddenly refer to Naomi the way she refers to herself. By continuing to call her Naomi instead of Mara, the biblical author, like Christ, upholds the truth that we are not the sum of the worst things that have happened to us.

Where we find ourselves will never change who God died for us to be. Mended and whole. Soft and pliable. Honest and true. In Christ, our pain is stripped of having the final say. In Christ, love speaks a louder word over the names we give ourselves in our lowest Mara moments.

Denial Won't Make Us Soft

Naomi doesn't enter Bethlehem proclaiming lies or jargon she knows will set her friends at ease. She doesn't find refuge in the mirage. And she doesn't stand on a hope that consists of fragments of her glorified denial. As tired as she is from the long journey and the sorrowful years, she makes it known that even though she's home, she's not the same. Naomi gets this much right: she does not dress her despair with a fake narrative. And this is wisdom we can learn from her.

In our longing to be rescued from the pain, we can refuse to be candid about the reality of our situation. We try to stop the pain by settling into a mirage in the middle of the desert. We decide that the desert is not a hallway to walk through but a home to abide in, even though there's nothing to sustain us there.

But the miracle of being made soft begins the moment we tell the truth. There will be times and seasons we must give ourselves over to the truth that we are not as soft as we want or were created to be. Like sanctification, the process of being made holy, becoming soft is a process and a journey we settle into as we live on this side of eternity. It is a journey that begins with the first step of naming the hard edges, the bitterness, and the suffering that threaten to strip us of our hope that we will see "the goodness of the LORD in the land of the living" (Ps. 27:13 NIV).

We don't receive the grace of softening by gaslighting ourselves. We don't heal through pretending. A debt was paid to make us worthy, in and through Christ, of receiving a healing that does not placate our pain nor demand bearing false witness of our suffering.

The truth of what you've been through is etched on your soul. The multiple soul-shattering miscarriages. The abuse you endured by people who spoke of the same God you're told can heal. The betrayal that mocked your worth. The marriage you couldn't save in your prayer closet. The endings

35

that came like a gut punch, and the suffering that came in wave after wave. But refusing to name the hurt that hides within doesn't make you softer. If anything, denial only fertilizes the soil where our resentment toward God can grow.

Naomi's journey has only just begun, but naming her pain is a start, just as it can be a start for all of us. Honesty itself is not the miracle, but it's what Christ uses to bring us to a place of restoring our hard hearts into pliable hearts of flesh. Honesty is what *opens* us up to the miraculous work of God.

You are made for more. Your identity cannot be reduced to the sum of your affliction. You are made for a greater life than one spent pretending shards from this broken world haven't cut into your spirit, your belief, and your faith. You are created to have courage that makes you brave enough to tell the truth, name your pain, and offer your groans to the heavens with faith that God will enter in.

I've encountered many Mara moments that held potential for either further hardening or the promise of a type of tenderness that comes when God's presence dwells in honesty. When I returned once again to my hometown in Colorado, two years after having my daughter and after my marriage ended, I decided to create a refuge by masquerading around with a smile that would keep my heart out of reach. I didn't want to be touched by the warmth of the community or my Creator.

One Sunday an old friend settled next to me in the darkened church auditorium. I could sense a question was brewing in her brain, so I braced myself and prepared to recite my prepared script. She began, "If you don't mind me asking, what brought you back?" I had been asked this question before, but this time something was different. This time her words carried the spirit of Naomi's friends, who compassionately bore witness to the way in which her pain had marked her and introduced her before she said a word.

I met my friend's eyes and noticed how they were kind and bright even with the house lights dimmed. And somehow, without hesitation, I told her the truth of why I was sitting next to her in a familiar place feeling anything but familiar within myself. She rubbed my leg and let the silence breathe between us as she held back tears. Then she whispered, "I'm so sorry, and I can't imagine what you're going through. But I am so happy you are home."

The heavens didn't open. The voice of God didn't suddenly proclaim all was well. Her touch didn't immediately heal all my pain. In fact, I don't think I mustered up more than a "thank you" before service began. My heart was still hard—and yet something was changing. I did not receive the miracle of being made soft at that moment, but I was the recipient of the miracle of being made *safe*. Safe enough to pour out the story that had been sealing up my heart in order to make room for God's hand to do its work. And through that moment of safe disclosure, an invitation was extended to me to be brave enough to tell the truth and to dare to believe that my story wasn't over. My friend saw me in my pain, and her witness gave me permission to let go of both the mirages and my Mara moments to fully see my own pain and be loved in it. In that moment she breathed on the dying embers of my hope, and I found the courage to keep going on the journey of becoming soft.

Go and Be Made Well

There's no list of bullet points we can check off as we heal toward softness. The process of being made soft is built on telling the truth about the lives we have lived: the good, the hard, the bitter, the sweet. It is only by telling the truth that we destroy the mirages we've projected onto our situations and testify to the lives we have lived, the pain we have endured, the losses we have faced. And it is only by coming out of denial that we are made well.

You are not made well by pretending to be well.

When Jesus healed the woman with the issue of blood (Matt. 9:20–22), the ten lepers (Luke 17:11–19), and the blind man (Mark 10:46–52), He did not proclaim that their ability to fake it had made them well. Each time He declared that their faith had made them well. And this faith was not their confidence in their ability to do for themselves or to act as if they were not in need. It was their confidence in Jesus's ability to restore them back to their true selves.

You are also not made well by being named by what made you unwell.

Your true self is one with a soft heart. Your healing comes through your honesty regarding the things that have broken your heart and your hope that you are not your brokenness. And no matter where this book has landed in your story, the truth is that all you need is to be confident that God can soften what the world has hardened. That God can restore your warped perception of what living softly means. Your healing journey begins with the understanding that God can do more with your honesty than He can with your mirages, and He longs to rescue you from the bondage of being named by your pain.

3

OLDER BROTHER SYNDROME

How a False Sense of Faith Hardens Your Heart

I grew up hearing my pastor call for the prodigals at least once a month. The person on the keyboard would play a melody to match the emotions in that moment, and you could hear the wails and whimpers of mothers weeping over their "lost sons and daughters."

For many of us, that is what Jesus's parable of the prodigal son in Luke 15 is about—the lost son being restored to the father who never stopped longing for his son's homecoming. But this chapter in Luke continues three parables (the lost sheep, the lost coin, and the lost son) that are told as a direct response to the Pharisees' and scribes' complaint about Jesus keeping company with sinners (v. 2). These parables aren't meant only for those who considered themselves wayward and too far from the grip of grace but for those who look at the lost with contempt.

When we think of the Pharisees in the text, we don't liken them to those who uphold the law with tenderness. These experts in the law are so callous toward the things of God that they can't perceive His presence in their midst. The state of their hearts prohibits them from recognizing Jesus in the miracles, signs, and wonders He performs and the wisdom He speaks. So, I can imagine their dissatisfaction with how the younger son, who seemingly squandered the riches of his father, is welcomed back so easily. Resigned to return as a servant, the prodigal is instead received as a son.

For the Pharisees, who are listening with a critical spirit, it's a reminder that those who are lost cannot be stripped of their identity of sonship. And as if that isn't shocking enough, Jesus then takes His listeners from the scene inside the house with the younger brother, where the story could have ended—and tells the narrative of the older brother, who might be the *real* lost son of the story.

The older son has been in the field all day, as usual. It had been quite some time since his younger brother had left with his share of their inheritance from their father. Thinking of how foolish it was of his brother to take what was his prematurely, he smiles to himself at the thought of receiving what is due to him in the future. He will work and wait until then. The sun is sinking into the hills as he heads toward his father's house. As he draws nearer, the sounds of music and dancing catch him off guard. Why did this ordinary day call for celebration? Still a distance from the house, the oldest son calls out to one of the servants and asks what's going on. Filled with excitement, the servant replies that the younger son has returned.

The older brother burns with rage. His throat grows hot as he catches a glimpse of the dancing through the window.

The music triggers his indignation, and he refuses to enter the house.

> Then he became angry and didn't want to go in. So his father came out and pleaded with him. But he replied to his father, "Look, *I have been slaving many years for you*, and I have never disobeyed your orders, yet *you never gave me a goat so that I could celebrate with my friends.*" (Luke 15:28–29)

Jesus uses the older brother to expose the hearts of the listening Pharisees. The older brother represents the contempt that can grow when our hands are faithful but our hearts are far from the Lord. He is lost in his own works; his heart has grown hard as he lived in the father's house but distanced himself from the father's heart.

Of all the taboos in the Christian community, this one may be the most prominent. It's an unwritten rule, one many consider to be the eleventh commandment: Thou shalt not be mad at God. And yet we've all experienced moments when we've raised our fists to the sky, angry at what we believe God is doing or not doing in our lives. But behind our self-righteous anger are beliefs that keep us in the Father's house but separate from the intimacy of dwelling with the Father. We become angry when we believe we are slaves and not children of God, we feel owed, and we lack the softness to celebrate the return of those who were once lost.

Saints Aren't Slaves

I'm the oldest of five, and for much of my life I played the role of substitute mom. My parents bragged about me being an easy baby, who then became an easy adolescent and inevitably an easy adult. But being the easy child lacked ease. I was constantly operating under the fear that my parents' love for me would vanish the moment I messed up. And that, naturally, flowed into my relationship with God. I would spend hours in my room writing confession after confession of all the things I did wrong, terrified that I had failed and fallen too far from His grace and believing I needed to prove I could do better. I rarely experienced the rest of being His. To me, affection was something I had to strive for and achieve.

I found more comfort in doing for God than in being for God. Closeness to the Father meant shedding these beliefs, which had carried me for so many years. I was certain that the closer people got to me the less they would love me. I can empathize with the older brother. Underneath self-righteous anger is almost always a deep longing to be fully seen and fully loved.

The older brother was a son, but he reduced himself to a slave. His obsession with his deeds stripped him of his true identity as beloved. And because he lived with this distortion, he also lived as if the inheritance was a prize to be won and not his father's gift. The older brother worked hard. He spent his life laboring with dedication to receive the reward on the other side *of his own goodness*. He tied his work to his own virtue. When he became weary and faint, he wasn't built up by *who he was* to his father but by *what he could do* for his father. He used his labor to sustain his sense of belonging.

After all, believing we belong is risky business.

It's a risk to believe God loves us based on His perfect love and not on our attempts at perfection.

It's a risk to believe we don't have to earn belonging in
the family of God.

It's a risk to believe we are fully seen *and* fully loved.

But when we cannot accept the unconditional love of
Christ for the wholeness of our humanity, our hearts tend
to harden. We tend to conclude that Immanuel, *God with us*,
always carries an asterisk. We come to believe God is with us
sometimes—when or if we've been good. We define goodness
by our own standards: how long we spend in the field, how
often we sacrifice, how we let the sun beat down on our faces
as we toil faithfully. We then approach God with hearts that
have hardened despite our proximity to Him.

Like the older brother's, our anger causes us to reduce our
identity from child of God to slave. We point to our calloused
hands gained from working not as sons but as slaves in the
fields of the Father. We present ourselves as suffering servants
but deny the form of suffering that brings glory to God. Instead
we want to be deemed righteous for suffering toward our own
glorification. We remind God of all the pain, all the wounds, all
the blows we took because we wanted to be the "good spouse"
or the "good church member" or the "good employee."

Slaves gain favor based on their own merit.

Sons receive favor based on who they belong to.

I'm not one to say we have any reason to be angry with
God, as He is gracious and kind despite our lack of understanding. But anger is a secondary emotion. It's a neon sign
that points to the real feeling underneath. Most of us who
think we are secretly carrying anger are likely carrying hurt.

Underneath the attempt to manipulate God's hand and gain His attention through our performance is the calcified doubt that we can't belong as ourselves.

Generating favor based on who we are may seem like a better offer than receiving favor based on who God is. Hiding under the shadow of the wings of our works, our attempts at perfection, our pride, and our self-righteousness might give us the sensation of refuge—but never the satisfaction. Never the security. Never the peace. Here is the truth I hope you do not miss: your identity in Christ is not hanging in the balance. It's not up for negotiation, and it's not something you can earn by working harder.

We must fight to see ourselves rightly: as saints and not slaves, heirs and not house servants. We must fight to see God rightly: not as an enslaver who keeps a ledger filled with all the works that balance out our debt but as an unconditionally loving Father. If we don't, we'll approach the throne of grace as if we are owed.

You Owe Me

I was a purity culture poster child. I read *I Kissed Dating Goodbye* when I was thirteen, and Elisabeth and Jim Elliot's love story in *Passion and Purity* was a fairy tale to me. When I was fifteen, I attended a special ceremony to officially commit my purity to the Lord. Dressed in a lavender gown, I signed a contract pledging my virginity to God and received a silver band as a purity ring I wore on my wedding finger. I would write notes to my future husband and dream of our life together. I took a lot of pride in the fact that I never had a boyfriend and never kissed anyone. I was saving myself to get the dream. I was saving myself to earn my perfect love story. When I met my husband, he became my first everything.

When my marriage unraveled from infidelity, I honestly felt robbed. This wasn't supposed to be the life of someone who did everything right before marriage. I did what I was told to do, yet it didn't keep my husband from doing right by me. My good deeds didn't produce what I thought they would. I held up my end of the bargain by being the "pure Christian girl," yet it seemed like God didn't hold up His end.

It was a ridiculous conclusion, but one we've all reached in some way. We keep His commandments because it's what we're expected to do. But we obey with our own expectations. After a while we approach the Father to collect what we feel we are owed.

> *I "saved" myself for marriage, so why did my spouse have an affair?*
>
> *I served faithfully at church for years, so why didn't I get that promotion?*
>
> *I am a good person and I've done good things, so why didn't I get what I asked for?*

We are not hardened by our pursuit of holiness. But we are subtly and surely hardened when we put our hand to the plow with transactional intent. What was a blessing of inheritance became the older brother's burden of proof that he was good enough to get what he believed he deserved. And don't we do the same? Our hearts are prone to grow hard when we worship a god we've created in our own image. Or worse, when we pursue God as only a means to an end, deciding He is not enough.

When our obedience doesn't lead to the outcome we deem we've earned by our sacrifice, our bewilderment makes us hard. Our gaze becomes cloudy with disillusionment. And whoever comes under it, whether God or other people, is covered with the sense of judgment we use to protect our hearts from the hurt of misunderstanding the nature of God.

We cover our hearts with a high sense of self and a low sense of our shortcomings. We scream at God that we deserve what we are owed, because we are the faithful son and have "never disobeyed" (Luke 15:29). The indignation we feel deceives us into thinking that the sweat we dropped while faithfully working in the field is equivalent to the blood Jesus shed on Calvary. It is blasphemy disguised as virtue.

Here's the truth: God doesn't force us to love Him, and we cannot force His hand to make Him love us more. And as we experience the love of God, we are moved to respond to it with obedience. Blessings flow from His hand, and we can't manipulate His grip. And that is good news.

That Son of Yours

The last symptom of "older brother syndrome" is seen when the older son begins to talk about his brother:

> You never gave me even a young goat so I could celebrate with my friends. But when this son of yours who has squandered your property with prostitutes comes home, you kill the fattened calf for him! (v. 30 NIV)

He first refers to his brother as "this son of yours" in an open display of distancing. We are prone to do this as well; when we uphold a theology that preserves division, we can look at our spiritual siblings as the other. We can tell ourselves that though they belong to God, they are not, as Gwendolyn Brooks writes, "our magnitude and bond."[1]

The older brother then attempts to discredit the celebration by bringing up the younger brother's sins. While he is correct that the younger brother did squander his inheritance, he assumes the worst without any idea what he'd been through. He's unaware the younger brother had been afflicted by a severe famine. Or that his brother had been so hungry and in need that he took a job that would be considered offensive and unclean as a Jewish person by working with swine. He has no idea that no one offered him anything and that he returned to the father's home willing to be a slave.

Older brother syndrome is dangerous because of its ability to strip us of compassion. The older brother was envious of the fattened calf slaughtered in honor of the prodigal son, unaware that it was likely his first meal in a long time. He couldn't see the mercy of God on display as they threw a party that could have been a funeral. His envy so clouded his vision that he believed God was holding out on him.

But God in His goodness leaves the door open for both of His sons. In His extravagant love, the Father runs to the prodigal son as he returns—and He comes out to plead with the older son sitting outside His home.

Soft and Holy

I want to affirm those who have lived a life devoted to Christ. Your pursuit of righteousness is, of itself, not the makings of a hard heart. The God-fearing Pharisee is regarded well in the

Writings: "The fear of the LORD leads to life, and whoever has it rests satisfied; he will not be visited by harm" (Prov. 19:23 ESV). Our awe of God will always lead to our desire to respond rightly. And we cannot call any pursuit of righteousness evidence of the spirit of the Pharisee. We are called to holiness. We are called to obedience and a life of surrender. But a heart intent on earning and being owed God's love is not softer than one who lets other loves lead them away.

When we abide in Christ, we receive the miracle of being soft as we are being refined through obedience. Our "yes" to Him spills out because of our love for Him. And while we enjoy His favor and gather what He chooses to bless us with, it doesn't replace knowing Him. Knowing God gives us the reward of knowing Him. We cannot be soft if we treat our relationship with Christ like a transaction or dodge being known for the sake of being praised for our works.

There is a better way. One better than pretending the rags of our self-righteousness can be stitched together into something that moves His heart.

God longs to soften you with the truth that you cannot manipulate His hand nor earn His love. He longs to melt your heart of stone with the same words He offered the older brother burning with rage: "You are always with me, and everything I have is yours" (v. 31). Delight cures the heart that is sick with self-righteousness. Any saint who regards themselves as a mere slave can reclaim their identity as they enjoy the Father and dwell in His house.

The invitation is extended. And when you accept it, you are free from the lie that the only way to know God is through a transaction. You are free from the lie that following Jesus with the intention to simply know Him is not enough. You are not meant to claw your way to the love that is offered as a gift with no strings attached. And you don't have to hide behind the false narrative that you can consider yourself better than others and call your pride holiness.

God comes to you as you sit outside His house with the hope that you'd be brave enough to enter His house as a beloved child. That you'd be courageous enough to resist the sin of self-righteousness that produces complacency, to be holy as He is holy, and to be soft of heart as Christ is soft. That you would learn to walk in the holiness that never outgrows the need for God's mercy and the delight in His love. His is a love that we cannot earn with bloodied knuckles or calloused skin, trying to prove we deserve the inheritance of the cross. His is a love that softens us with the radical truth that we are recipients of what we could never barter from God: a sacred softening that begins when we allow the Good News to stand on His goodness, not our own.

4

WHALES AND WEEDS

Cynicism's Subtle Attack on Your Heart

I've always been a romantic. I was the girl who had her wedding board on Pinterest before she had a boyfriend. I would create imaginary scenarios in every area of my life. I was obsessed with romanticizing my life before it was a trendy aesthetic on social media. My hope was up because it hadn't yet been broken down. I buried stories of love deep in my heart and was convinced that finding "the one" would be filled with fireworks and butterflies.

I wanted the fairy-tale version of faith, of marriage, of motherhood. And instead I got life. I longed for a fairy-tale marriage, and instead lived in a marriage filled with dysfunction. I longed for a fairy-tale birthing experience, and instead almost lost my son and labored alone with my daughter.

Soon hoping wasn't worth the risk. I no longer asked myself, *What if it all works out?* and instead looked to the future asking, *How quickly will I be let down?* I was certain I could protect myself by assuming the worst—in life, in people, and in God. Instead of allowing God to cover my disappointment, I began to cover it myself.

I stopped trusting in hope and befriended cynicism instead. Cynicism isn't merely living with a healthy level of suspicion. By definition, cynicism is the operating belief that no one is sincere and that people are only interested in themselves.[1] Cynicism is the antithesis of wonder. It's a form of skepticism birthed when we are let down—by others, by the things of this world, and by God.

It's not difficult to spot our cynicism with the world. Most of us walk around with a "healthy" level of cynicism that protects us from naivete. But our spirits are not protected by cynicism in the same way our physical selves are. When unchecked in the heart, cynicism becomes a spiritual disease. It's the kind of cancerous sin that erodes the heart slowly but efficiently. We *grow* cynical. Or, rather, cynicism grows in us.

I'm not sure there's a kid in the world who doesn't love dandelions in the spring. Every mother has received a bouquet of the dainty yellow flower and placed it in her hair. The thing is, dandelions are weeds. And their long taproots can cause trouble for gardeners. We think cynicism is a flower of wisdom, but it is a weed. We think cynicism is a flower of maturity, but it is a weed. We think cynicism is a flower of discernment, but it is a weed. And when we keep the "dandelions of cynicism" in the garden of our hearts, calling them what they are not, their roots continue to grow deeper and stronger.

Cynicism is as deceptive as it is subtle. And you may feel inclined to skip this chapter, which claims the roots of this "dandelion" are actively hardening your heart. But I'd implore you to see if you relate to these symptoms first:

- You expect the worst.
- When someone tells you to stop and smell the roses, you quickly point out the thorns.
- You downplay the work of the Holy Spirit.
- You roll your eyes at happy people and tell yourself they're secretly miserable.
- You distort the gift of discernment from seeing the good to hunting for the bad.

Cynicism is not the character of a mature Christian, it's the defense mechanism of a wounded one.

Those of us who have grown up in the church or have walked with the Lord for many years are the most vulnerable to this sinister sin. We mature as we should, moving from the milk to the meat of our faith, leaving childish things behind and engaging with the text with seasoned spirits. We grow in Christ. We grow in understanding. We grow in the good things of following God and pursuing holiness. But if we are not careful, a good thing can grow into an idol. An idol that sends our hearts into a cold state—unable to love God and love others. Unable to partake in a faith that is alive. If we are not careful, we will find ourselves running from the voice of God the same way Jonah did.

It's Not about a Whale

"And then, Mommy, Jonah got ate up by a whale," my son explained from the backseat of our car after school. Every month, his school focused on a different character of the Bible, and that month it was Jonah.

"So, what is the story of Jonah about, honey?" I asked, to keep the conversation going. One, because I will never pass up the opportunity to hear a child retell a story from the Bible that I already know. And two, because my son's love language is telling me the intricate details of his day, and my decision to listen would register with him as a display of love.

I glanced at him through the rearview mirror, and he rolled his eyes—a reaction I didn't expect considering I was doing him a favor by pretending I hadn't heard this story 19,679 times.

"Mommy, you know. He didn't listen to God. That's why he got ate up!"

If we were honest, most of us would give the same synopsis about Jonah. God told him to go to Nineveh. Jonah didn't want to go, so he fled, and in doing so he was "eaten" by a giant fish. He inevitably got spat out by the fish after deciding to obey God, and then he headed to Nineveh. The moral of the story is simple: obey God or get "ate up."

But the book of Jonah, according to many scholars, is what we would consider a satire that isn't about the whale or even Jonah running away. Jonah is a prophet who has a spirit like that of the older brother from Jesus's parable in Luke 15. He's deeply hypocritical, and he flees God not because he doesn't want to do what God said but because he doesn't want God to display His character to the Ninevites. He doesn't want God to show mercy to a city he believes is beyond mercy. Jonah's heart runs deep with roots that keep him spouting God's goodness while staying skeptical about how it could be poured out on those Jonah deems undeserving.

It's sometimes difficult to identify cynicism because it masquerades as intellect married to mature faith. Cynicism impersonates righteousness and discernment, and it does so to perpetuate our own desire to judge what we do not understand or prefer. Jonah is a prophet of God. His life is centered around the ministry of doing what God tells him to do in Nineveh. But somewhere along the way, his "rationality" leads to his rebellion.

Jonah's rebellion centers around his own limited and self-serving understanding of God. According to Jonah, the people in Nineveh do not deserve the mercy of God, an attitude that turns Jonah from remembering that he also has not deserved to receive God's mercy to believing he is a better judicator of the Ninevites than God. In the end, *the book of Jonah is not about the whale.* Though Jonah possesses the same dramatic antics I've seen in my three-year-old when she doesn't want to do something, it's not about a grown man having a tantrum over what God asks of him. This is a story about how cynicism can transform a heart. Jonah is satisfied with a God who would show mercy to him, but could not and would not witness the mercy of God toward others.

Cynicism did to Jonah what it does to all of us: it renders our understanding of God smaller and smaller.

Bigger and Bigger

In C. S. Lewis's book *Prince Caspian*, the four Pevensie children return to the land of Narnia to find it is a very different place.[2] Narnia has been overrun by the Telmarines and is now ruled by the tyrant Lord Mirza, who has plans to murder his nephew, Prince Caspian, the rightful heir to the throne. The

Pevensie children join Prince Caspian to defeat Lord Mirza. Throughout the book, the youngest child, Lucy, is repeatedly overlooked and dismissed by her siblings. Aslan, the Lion that represents Christ, has yet to return to Narnia. Prince Caspian and the three other Pevensie children are convinced Aslan will not return and the battle will be theirs to fight alone. But Lucy remains expectant that the Lion will return.

As the group continues their journey, Lucy spots Aslan in the thick of the woods. She shouts with excitement and tries to tell her siblings she just saw him, but they don't believe her. Dismissed again, Lucy cries bitterly as they all prepare to sleep.

In the still of the night, Lucy is awakened by a voice saying her name. As she follows the voice, she sees Aslan's silhouette in the moonlight. She takes in the stature and majesty of the great Lion and concludes that the years have made him bigger. Aslan responds that it is not him but simply her perspective of him that has grown.

This beautiful storytelling reminds me of a moment in which I found myself staring at my children as they looked out the window. In their youth, the world was so big. So vast. So full of wonder. As I watched them taking it all in, I realized that as they grew, the world would grow smaller and smaller. One day, the awe of watching a squirrel scurrying up a tree or the shapes made by the clouds would fade away. One day, the magical would become mundane. But here, as Lucy sits with Aslan, convinced he has grown, we see that beautiful paradox that is God's kingdom at play.

As we get older, things in the natural world become smaller, less impressive. But in the spiritual world, the opposite is true. The evidence of spiritual growth is that, as we get closer to God, our awe of Him becomes bigger. Sanctification produces a sense of awe, and awe is the antidote for our cynicism. A cynical heart is a heart untouched by wonder.

In Paul Tripp's *Instruments in the Redeemer's Hands*, he discusses constant conflict within believers to offer people principles, strategies, and concepts of redemption instead of the Redeemer Himself. A heart plagued by cynicism, somewhere along the way, believes that God isn't enough. And that knowing Him is secondary to knowing *about* Him.

Maturing in the Lord is not simply the act of collecting knowledge. It is also not a sense of superiority that leads us to hoard knowledge to prove we belong. Maturity is not growing suspicious but growing in astonishment. As we grow in Christ, our awe, wonder, esteem, and reverence for Christ grow too.

There is a duality of cynicism we wade through as believers. On the one hand, the world and all its disappointments and falsities produce a cynicism that leads us to desire the hope found in the gospel. Those of us who cling to the Word are likely those who long for a better world and cannot find it in the things of this world.

Underneath our cynicism is a hopeful romantic who was knocked off their feet by a cruel reality.

The False Shelter of Cynicism

Most believers who struggle with cynicism were once wrapped in wonder, fascinated by the Word of God, and eager to know more. We were treasure hunters living off the ecstasy of finding nuggets buried in the Scriptures. Until the world let us down by not being safe enough to hold our wonder. None of us can walk through life unscathed by events that can birth cynicism in our hearts. And somewhere along the way, we realize disappointment with God feels much like disappointment without God.

It's different but strangely the same.

After Jonah runs from God and finds himself in the belly of the fish, he decides to choose obedience. The fish vomits him out, and Jonah makes the three-day trek to Nineveh. When he arrives, he tells the Ninevites to turn from their evil ways and back to God before they are destroyed. The warning reaches the king, and he proclaims a fast and responds to the voice of the Lord. God sees their repentance, shows Nineveh compassion, and does not bring the destruction He threatened. You might assume the story ends there, and that Jonah rejoices in the fact that these people are restored. You would think that as a prophet, a man devoted to declaring messages that provoke a response, he would find himself praising God for their swift repentance. But Jonah seethes at this display of compassion. "To Jonah this seemed very wrong, and he became angry" (Jon. 4:1 NIV).

When we case our hearts with the armor of cynicism, we find ourselves observing what is beautiful and calling it wrong. What we once viewed with eyes filled with wonder we now observe with suspicion. We curse the things of God that once delighted us. Jonah's anger is built on his belief that he knows better than God. He's called to proclaim the Word of the Lord, but he takes it upon himself to decide who is worthy or unworthy of receiving mercy.

Jonah then confesses why he ran. It wasn't because he didn't feel like going to Nineveh. It wasn't because he was afraid the people of Nineveh would disregard his warning.

Jonah ran because he was afraid God would respond according to His character and not according to Jonah's contempt. Jonah ran because he knew God would be "gracious and compassionate . . . slow to anger and abounding in love" (v. 2 NIV) to *them.* He knew God would be God to *those people.*

So God asks Jonah a question: "Is it right for you to be angry?" (v. 4). We each must reckon with this question as well. Are we boiling with rage because of God's righteousness or because of our self-righteousness?

Jonah doesn't respond and instead prepares a shelter for himself, on the east side of the city, to watch what would happen to Nineveh. He, like a cynic, is consumed with peering into and passing judgment on the lives of others. His suspicion overcomes his understanding of what he knows to be true of God—that He cannot operate outside of His character. God had made it clear that He would relent and not bring destruction. But Jonah isn't convinced. His heart is so distanced from God's true nature that he's hoping for the worst. He has become so riddled with contempt that he prefers to be a spectator of judgment rather than a participant of grace.

It's easy to operate as a modern-day Jonah. We scroll on our phones as spectators. We watch with no intention of getting into the thick of it all. We consume content made by critics and wonder why we're more enraged than empowered.

Those of us who have let the root of cynicism burrow itself into our hearts have attempted to create a shelter made with the leaves of our suspicion and judgment, only to find no relief. We think that as we sit and cast judgment on those who don't *really* love God or aren't *truly* followers of Jesus, we can establish our own sense of security.

As Jonah sits on the hill, simmering and waiting for God to destroy Nineveh, the Lord makes a leafy plant sprout up from the ground. The shelter Jonah has made for himself is clearly not enough, and this plant provided by the Lord eases Jonah's discomfort in the heat of the sun. But the next day, God sends a worm to eat the plant until it withers. Then He sends a scorching hot wind, and Jonah, now exposed, grows so faint that he begs God to let him die. In Jonah 4:9, God asks Jonah the same question: "Do you have a right to be angry?" (NABRE).

Jonah replies with a passionate yes.

He tells God that his anger concerning the plant is so righteous that it was consuming him to the point of desiring death. Quite dramatic. And yet, God remains with Jonah and gently corrects the errant prophet, addressing the truth behind his rage:

> But the LORD said, "You have been concerned about this plant, though you did not tend it or make it grow. It sprang up overnight and died overnight. And should I not have concern for the great city of Nineveh, in which there are more than a hundred and twenty thousand *people* who cannot tell their right hand from their left—and also many animals?" (vv. 10–11 NIV)

The sinister nature of cynicism is that it elevates the plant that provides *personal* shelter above the person who is just as in need of shelter as we are. A heart hardened by cynicism doesn't see an image bearer as they spout off criticism. They are so blinded by their contempt that people are never more important to them than a point to be made or a suspicion to be proven. Should God not concern Himself with a people more than Jonah concerned himself with the plant? When we navigate through this world more skeptical than hopeful, we strip ourselves of the ability to see people as worthy recipients of mercy on the merit of Christ alone. We consider people too far gone, while God tries to show us the span of His reach.

The Courage to Trust Hope Again

So, what is the cure for the heart unwell with cynicism? What is the remedy for the ache that comes with a skeptical heart? How do we walk the tightrope of knowledge and wonder?

There is an aspect of Jonah's story that is often missed. We can conclude that one reason Jonah flees is because he fears the Ninevites. And he has every reason to. Nahum 3 gives us a glimpse into just how wicked they are:

> Woe to the city of blood,
>   full of lies,
> full of plunder,
>   never without victims! . . .
> Charging cavalry,
>   flashing swords
>   and glittering spears!
> Many casualties,
>   piles of dead,
> bodies without number,
>   people stumbling over the corpses. (vv. 1, 3 NIV)

It's understandable that when Jonah hears the word *Nineveh*, he tells God to "Get somebody else to do it!" But there is another reason Jonah doesn't want to go. If I could offer a modern-day interpretation, we could imagine Jonah as a Jewish man during World War II being told by God, "I'm going to bring terrible judgment on Nazi Germany. I want you to go to Berlin and tell the people there to repent."

Here's what I need you to know: I empathize with your cynicism. I understand what it's like to experience the kind of loss and letdown that makes it hard to feel alive. I can relate to Jacob in Genesis 45 when his sons inform him that, after all these years, Joseph was alive. "But Jacob didn't believe them, because he had become cynical [lit. his heart had become numb]" (Gen. 45:26 ISV). I can relate to Jonah, cynical after witnessing the evils people are capable of. I can relate to the truth J. A. Marx writes that "Cynicism comes from repeated wounding, from hope deferred, trust broken, doused optimism, and shaken beliefs."[3]

I sympathize that there are things that have made you cynical, but you were made for more.

The story of Jonah ends with a cliffhanger. Jonah persists that he has every right to be angry about the plant. Then God responds—and the book of Jonah ends. We don't know what happens to Jonah. We don't know if he wrestles with his contempt and lets hope win on that hill. We don't know if he continues to simmer with anger waiting for something that would never happen. But what we do know is that God has the final say. That the book of Jonah ends with an invitation that softens the heart of the cynic—an invitation to allow God to finish the conversation our cynicism started.

When we let our wounds have the final say, we mute hope's ability to speak over our limited perspective. Yet when we make the courageous choice to give Christ the last word, we rip up the roots of cynicism.

There is a better way. And God is in pursuit of your cold, cynical heart. He'll send a big fish to swallow you before you drown. He'll send a tree to cover you before you wither under the hot sun. He'll pursue you despite your defiance.

When we let Christ enter our disappointment, our wonder and hope for life are preserved. And sometimes the fight to stay soft looks like a determined walk back to the wonder and awe of God in a dim and dull world. Sometimes we wage war against the callousness of cynicism by taking the risk to hope again.

In the same way our hearts gradually fade into the abyss of cynicism, the return back to wonder may feel slow. It may feel like dipping your toe in the pool you've longed to plunge into for months but aren't quite ready to yet. It may feel like casting hope when you're more inclined to cast judgment. I pray God wraps you in wonder and serenades you with delight. That you would live with your breath less constricted and your heart freer to see the goodness of humanity and the goodness that is God.

5

FORGET THEE NOT

How Remembrance Is the Soil of Your Soft Heart

I was at my end. My wall was covered with sticky notes of all colors, neon square patches scribbled with things I needed to remember. My desk was cluttered with the second planner I had purchased for the year, convinced that my inability to recall important dates was the planner's fault and not my own. It had become so bad I couldn't recall what I had for dinner the night before. Things were slipping through the cracks at the same rate that my shame was overcoming me.

I could not remember anything.

It took months for me to sit down with a therapist and tell her how my forgetfulness felt: exceptional. At first I'd considered it as the byproduct of "mom brain" or aging. I blamed all the factors that naturally make it hard to remember, and yet I eventually had to admit it seemed my forgetfulness was abnormal and I should get a professional opinion. I listed my symptoms, and after a few sessions I received a label that strangely gave me peace: *inattentive attention deficit disorder*. One label, and my shame seemed to peel off. It was not my fault, but it was also me in the sense that I was wired to be exceptional at forgetting.

The truth about humanity is that we are all exceptional at forgetting. Research finds that about 56 percent of information is forgotten within an hour, 66 percent after a day, and 75 percent after six days.[1] Our natural bent is toward forgetfulness.

Considering how easily we forget what we had for dinner last week, it's no surprise that we operate with the same forgetfulness regarding God. And though this spiritual amnesia can seem harmless, Scripture shows us that it almost always leads to rebellion. In our failure to recall the reasons that have been proven to help us remain, we rebel against the God we once cried out to.

The Israelites found themselves troubled by the Midianites for seven years. The Midianites destroyed their crops and stole their livestock, leaving no food for the Israelites. So God, in His loving-kindness, raises up a judge to restore His people back to Himself and chooses Gideon to defeat the Midianites—but first an angel tells Gideon to destroy the altar of Baal, the Midianites' god, which God's people had begun worshiping. The Israelites are so angry that they want to kill Gideon. These people have witnessed God rescue them from Egypt only to forsake Him and seek refuge in a god made with their own hands. They are hardened to the point of rebellion, but God still sends Gideon to rescue them from their oppressor.

With only three hundred men, Gideon defeats the Midianites. A demonstration of God's glory is once again on display for a people who had witnessed it before. And the Israelites have peace in their land for forty years, the rest of Gideon's lifetime. But then Gideon dies, and his death marks the end of peace. The Israelites "set up Baal-Berith as their god and *did not remember* the LORD their God, who had rescued them from the hands of all their enemies on every side" (Judg. 8:33–34 NIV). Forty years of peace come to an end because the Israelites forget to remember God.

The Bible uses the word *remember* over three hundred and fifty times. If you include variations of the word, it becomes over five hundred and fifty times. The spiritual discipline of remembering what God has said, who He has proved to be, and who He promised to be keeps our hearts tender. And a soft heart is a sensitive heart. When we contend against the inclination to grow hard with the lie that we are forgotten, our spirits are kept open to God when He could otherwise be missed.

He Remembers

There is a deep misconception that the God of the Old Testament is one of wrath and fury. Many of us are walking around with this dangerous theological dichotomy of "good cop / bad cop" Triune God. Jesus the Son, the gracious Savior of the New Testament, is the good cop, and God the Father, the raging Judge in the sky, is the bad cop. To be fair, it can be easy to read about such events as the great flood that wipes out almost all of humanity and see God as the bad cop—and Jesus as the one sent to clean up the Father's image. But Jesus is not sent as God's PR, and throughout the Old Testament we see that God's heart toward humanity is always soft and kind. One way we can see this softness in the Scriptures is whenever we read that "God remembered."

The Hebrew word for remembering is *zakar*, and it's more than the mere act of recalling information. According to Jewish scholar Nahum Sarna, "In the Bible, 'remembering,' particularly on the part of God, is not the retention or recollection of a mental image, but a focusing upon the object of memory that results in action."[2] Because God cannot forget, when the text states that He remembers it is not the mental exercise of recall but rather a recollection that moves Him to action.

When God remembers, He responds.

God's *zakar* permeates the Old Testament. The first time we see this type of remembrance is in Noah's narrative in Genesis. God's heart is broken over the evil plaguing people. Humanity is hell-bent on rebelling and exploiting His grace. Evil is running rampant, and God makes the decision to begin again. Yet after bringing the deluge, "God *remembered* Noah" and "sent a wind over the earth, and the waters began to subside" (Gen. 8:1 BSB). It's God's remembrance of Noah that leads to Him stopping the waters that had poured for forty days.

When God is ready to destroy Sodom and Gomorrah, He *remembers* Abraham and rescues Lot (19:29). When God *remembers* Rachel, He hears her prayers and touches her womb (30:22). When the people of Israel groan from their slavery, crying out for deliverance, God hears them and *remembers* His covenant with Abraham, Isaac, and Jacob (Exod. 2:23–35). And as He *remembers* He sees the people of Israel in their oppression and commissions Moses with the burning bush (3:1–10). While Hannah is weeping bitterly to the Lord about bearing a son, Eli prophesies to her, "Go in peace, and may the God of Israel grant you what you have asked of him" (1 Sam. 1:17 NIV). When she's intimate with her husband, Elkanah, the Lord *remembers* her, and she conceives a son (vv. 19–20).

God's remembrance moves Him to move on our behalf. In His deity He cannot forget. It is not in His nature to be absent-minded.

And yet we've all felt like David did in Psalm 77:9—forgotten by God. We've all sat in seasons when we're convinced God is passing us by. But as A. W. Tozer writes, "What comes into our minds when we think about God is the most important thing about us."[3] If we think we are forgotten, we'll live as if we are forgotten. If we think God has overlooked us, we'll live our lives accepting the crumbs scattered by the enemy of our souls, because we think God's silence is indicative of His absence.

God has not forgotten you.

I hope you have the courage to fight for the softness that comes with reaching for that truth even when it feels untrue. All the times the people we love forget about us or overlook us have a way of informing our conclusions of God. We think because people tend to forget, God must as well. But there is an invitation to be made tender by the truth that we can never be forgotten by God.

Remember the Miracle of the Loaves

I journaled consistently for most of my adolescent life. But I would rarely finish a journal, as Barnes & Noble would always have a new one I had to have. Regardless, I was dedicated to pouring my thoughts out on those pages. One day, as I was cleaning out the storage in my parents' house, I found them all packed tightly in a cardboard box. I lowered myself onto the cement floor and began flipping through the pages. I've always been rather dramatic, and while I was certainly true to that characteristic in my adolescent journal entries, I noticed something else that made me realize how fickle I was when it came to remembrance. There were countless entries when my life was upside down and the act of remembering was a lifeboat. But when things were good, when I wasn't (in my arrogant belief) in need of saving, I'd forsake the intentional act of remembrance.

It's easy for a sense of comfort to numb our need to recall.

Our forgetfulness is evidence of our mortality. It's proof of our limitations that stand in stark contrast to the never-forgetful God. As we see in Scripture time and time again, when people forget, we respond to the silence, the hardship, and the storm not with the promises of God we can recall but with our own desire to soothe the chaos.

Our inability to remember what God has spoken and what we've seen to be true of His character doesn't necessarily lead to a hard heart. We are all prone to forget. Prone to wander from the monuments that serve as reminders of what God has done. But we must strive to remember because our forgetfulness will always bear its own kind of fruit. We tend to regard forgetfulness as a "small sin" that we can shake ourselves out of the moment we redirect our attention to God. But forgetfulness can become a practice, and one we must mindfully contend against. Moses warns the people of Israel of this type of chronic forgetfulness they (and we) are prone to:

Only be on your guard and diligently watch yourselves, so that you *don't forget the things your eyes have seen* and so that they don't slip from your mind as long as you live. (Deut. 4:9)

The fight to stay soft requires the fight to remember.

I can relate to the habitual forgetfulness of the Israelites. The desert has a way of giving us spiritual amnesia, and the wilderness can make us too weary to recall. But the warning remains because when we forget what we've witnessed that established God as trustworthy, we develop a desire to create our own source of trust. When God rescues His people from Egypt, when He parts the waters, when He causes manna to fall from heaven, He is displaying His glory to be gathered. Yet the moment God feels absent, the people fail to respond with remembrance but instead act with deliberate rebellion.

Before you distance yourself from the actions of the Israelites, I want you to consider how you recall the past. Do you look back with diligence to see God's hand in your memories? Or do you recall the presence of everything but Him? Do you fill the silence your doubt tries to squeeze into "the things your eyes have seen"? What we remember matters. We can look back at the journey behind us and recall all the things that "prove" God was absent—or we can, with the divine vision of His Spirit, look back and see the places in which He never left us and the hand He never lifted.

When God remembers, He responds, and when we remember, we are compelled to respond with the strength of our recollection. When we don't look back with the resolve to see God, we can ascribe our circumstances to His character.

The spiritual practice of remembrance is the act of gathering from the past. You gather the moments when you knew without a shadow of a doubt that God was present. You gather the moments when He intervened in your life and did what only He could do. And as you gather the evidence of God in your recollections, you receive the hope of knowing all God has done and will do again.

The Soil of the Soft

I grew up on Negro Spirituals. My dad would wake up the house on Saturday mornings with the voice of Mahalia Jackson signaling the start of our weekend cleaning routine. And there was one particular song he would sing with a smile on his face as he cooked one of the three things he knew how to make: chicken and rice, mashed potatoes, or spaghetti. In his deep baritone voice, he would sing, "Do Lord, oh do Lord, oh do remember me." My six-year-old self was more enamored by my dad's gentle singing than with the lyrics. But as I got older, this campfire-style song held a deep revelation.

He was singing a Negro Spiritual that had been passed down from generation to generation. If I'm being honest, I'll never fully comprehend the faith of my ancestors as they clung to God in the midst of their oppression. It's difficult not to burn with anger when I consider how they sang to a God who had forgotten them—not because He had truly forgotten them but because their captivity made it seem so. A seemingly forgotten people, believing, pleading to be remembered by God. Civil Rights activist and writer James Weldon Johnson articulates the beauty and tension of the Negro Spirituals that sustained those enslaved in his poem "O Black and Unknown Bards." The poem holds a line that strikes me to my core: "You sang far better than you knew."[4]

What my ancestors came to know was that their person-hood could be stripped by other people—they sang of better than what they came to know. They sang of hope and promise when all they knew was despair. They sang of the gaze of the Lord resting on them when all they knew was a life filled with eyes avoiding their being. They sang of remembrance when life whispered they'd been forgotten. And I believe they garnered a sense of strength by singing to believe, by pleading for what they longed to be true: *Do, Lord, remember me.* The very act of asking God to remember is an act of faith. It affirms the belief that God never forgets and will always act in accordance with who He is, even as we forget to recall His character.

Would you join me in this honest prayer?

God, remember the breath You breathed to make my being from the ash. Soul, remember God is your sustainer.

God, remember the promises You made to never leave. Soul, remember God is with you.

God, remember that You will bring hope to the hopeless. Soul, remember God is on His way.

Remembrance is the soil of a soft heart. It is the backbone of our faith. It is the heartbeat of our resilience. It strengthens our resolve to encounter the next hard thing because we recall how He brought us through the last hard thing. We contend for a soft heart *by* fighting to remember. And by fighting to believe we are not forgotten because God is always on the move. We contend to remember when life crushes us into a state of forgetfulness. And when we fail to remember, which we will, we can cling to the assurance of *being* remembered. We can stand on the rock of God's character when we struggle to recall His hand in our lives. We know the truth: He is not a God who forgets but a God who recalls His own promises and responds accordingly.

Remembrance is the soil that produces a harvest we can gather in our time of need. When we cannot see God's hand, we can unearth the bounty of what we've seen before. We can feast on our remembrance. We can nourish our weary souls. We can strengthen our brittle bones, fragile from the weight of seasons that seek to prove we've been forgotten.

Remember how you are remembered. Remember how He carried you after you collapsed and how He parted the seas you were confident you'd drown in. Sing from what you know, and sing into the future for what is yet to be true: that He remembers so we remember until we meet Him face-to-face.

6

JOSEPH'S TEARS

How Lamenting Makes You Tender

I still see the scene in my mind. It plays like a movie, interrupting my good days decades later. Of all the things I remember of that night, my exact age is not one of them. My dad was working late at the juvenile hall almost two hours away. He would drive in early in the morning, work an overnight shift, and then usually return while we were at school. Mom sat on this floral chair in the middle of our living room, and the light of the television illuminated our burgundy carpet. My younger sisters were absorbed in the show; they still lived in the luxury of being unaware. But I was watching—because I was always watching.

I was studying the way the air had grown thicker. I was panning the room to find the reason why whatever peace there was had dried up in an instant. I wondered until I knew. I saw that my mom's pupils were huge, her eyebrows to the sky. She was not ok, but to admit that would cause me to show my fear. And you can't play Mom and be a scared little girl at the same time (even though I wanted to).

She grabbed the corded phone on the glass table next to her chair, and I turned toward the screen, toward my sisters deep in the childhood I'd grown out of a few years back. Then I looked back at my mom, who I then realized was going deeper into whatever danger was rising in her mind, taking her far away from her three girls sitting on the carpet.

"Jesus is coming," she whispered. She said it again and again, in a way that felt both chilling and sacred. As if she were both certain and desperately trying to convince herself of this truth. "He's coming," she spoke into the phone. With the phone to her ear and her eyes on the television, my mom was clearly not listening to what her best friend was telling her over the phone. I couldn't hear, but I knew it didn't matter. My mom's friend couldn't rescue her from the waters she was drowning in with mere words from miles away. I knew I needed to act, and quickly. But before I could think of what to do, Mom hung up the phone, stood up, and began yelling at me.

"He's coming, Raia!"

I remained frozen, praying the wave would pass by quickly. Before—

"*Get dressed, Raia. Jesus is coming.* We've gotta meet Jesus. Jesus is coming."

And there it was. The wave I wished would pass me by was now hovering over me, mocking my childish prayers for my mom to be ok and for this unfair dynamic of playing substitute mother to come to an end. I knew she expected me to get both myself and my sisters ready. So I did what I knew to do: become the mom she couldn't be in that moment.

"He's coming. He's coming." Her words were a steady rhythm, a processional leading us to a moment that would forever mark my soul. She had us get into the car. We were old enough then, by early nineties standards, to not need car seats that required her assistance. But we were all still so young.

It was dark, which scared me even more. My dad was away. She had called him before we left on our quest to "meet our coming King." I knew he was concerned and likely had jumped into action and was even now making his way to us, but he wouldn't get here in time. Despite the deep figurative darkness we'd entered as my mom drove us away from our home, the full moon illuminated the sky enough that I could see the silhouette of the mountain range as my mom drove up a hill in the middle of the city—and then just . . . stopped. In the middle of traffic, she stopped the car right in the median. The fear I'd felt in the house as she repeated her mantra was nothing compared to this moment. Cars whizzed past, assuming we had stalled, I suppose.

Then it got even worse. My mother stepped out of the car.

As she stood in the middle of the street and raised her hands to the sky, it hit me that this was where she believed Jesus was coming. To meet her. To rescue her. To bring her home. My sisters had fallen asleep on the drive, lulled by the peace of being young enough to not fully understand. I grabbed the blanket lying on the floor and placed it over them, whispering "Everything's ok" before I climbed out to grab my mom.

My memory gets choppy after that, and much of what happened next is full of holes. Mom left the car. I covered my sisters. I left them and grabbed my mom to the sound of the empty whistling of the Colorado wind and the occasional honking horn. That seemed to rattle my mother back to reality. The paranoia stopped long enough for her to realize that Jesus wouldn't be coming back. Not there. Not that night.

Miraculously, we made it back home. My mom's CeCe Winans tape played as she drove in silence. My sisters' gentle snores calmed me down in their own way. And then we were home. My dad arrived. He tucked us into bed and asked if we were ok. I said yes to convince myself it was true. But that yes didn't take away what that moment did to me. It didn't keep me from declaring a silent oath before I closed my eyes: *God left me in the middle of a median, because that's where I belong. Girls like me don't get fairy tales. Girls like me don't get good things.*

In Viola Davis's memoir *Finding Me*, she shares a story of being on the set of *Suicide Squad* with Will Smith and having an aha moment. Smith asked Davis, "Who are you?" She was offended by the question and insisted she knew who she was. He asked her again, as if his repetition would bring clarity, and this time Davis asked what he meant. He responded, "Look, I'm always going to be that fifteen-year-old boy whose girlfriend broke up with him. That's always going to be me. So, who are you?"[1]

Davis pondered the question, and the answer hit her in the form of a memory: she is running home every day from a group of boys chasing her and hurling racial slurs at her heels. She then answered Smith, "I'm the little girl who would run after school every day in third grade because these boys hated me because I was . . . not pretty. Because I was . . . Black."[2]

Smith was the heartbroken teen.

Davis was the little girl running.

I was the scared girl in the middle of the street, under a full moon, convinced that no one was coming to protect me.

Further, I believed I was not worthy of protection. That moment formed the belief that my heart wasn't safe with the God who I believed deserted me that night. It wasn't safe because I was certain He didn't care enough to come to my rescue. And while His goodness pursued me and tried to lead toward the truth, every time I felt unprotected, that girl who'd pulled her mother back to the car tapped me on the shoulder and said, *What did I tell you?*

There are times when the natural and reasonable reaction to very real pain is to harden our hearts in self-protection, when we are hardened because we are touched by the actions of another. And these traumatic moments can cause us to spend the rest of our lives protecting the person who survived. That evening in the car with my mom was the day I decided that my heart could not be trusted in the Father's hand. And in my hurt, I lived waiting to be proven right. With every traumatic experience, my heart seized again as it added words to the story I was telling myself: *Girls like me don't get fairy tales. Girls like me don't get good things.*

Considering my past, it was no surprise that when I discovered infidelity and betrayal had made its way into my marriage story, the devastation only encouraged me to continue repeating this story.

One hot day in late summer, my heart broke and stiffened all at once. My two-year-old son was in my room as I paced in his. The window was open and a cool breeze blew into the room while I walked a figure eight as I listened to my husband on the other end of the phone. He had been gone for almost four months, and during the last few weeks my stomach had felt sick with suspicion. My husband became quiet on the other end of the line, and the silence felt like the proof I was both dodging and desperate for.

"Yes, Charaia. It's true."

"It" being what I had suspected for weeks. "It" being what left me unable to eat as my discernment continued to blare like a siren. "It" being betrayal that would soon become something I'd see many times over. But even though I knew this was the evidence of a choice he had made, the little girl stuck in the median whispered to me again, *Girls like me don't get good things.*

Tears to Make Tender

Maybe it's me, but I've never been happy with the telling of Joseph's story. I've sat under plenty of teaching that spoke of the trauma and pain he endured as merely stepping stones to his inevitable position as a leader. And though I am grateful for the ways in which this type of teaching serves as a reminder that God can work all things together for our good (Rom. 8:28), we sometimes fail to acknowledge the effect "all things" have on us. While God has proven and promised to take betrayal, harm, rejection, and hurt and piece them together into a tapestry for our good and His glory, this doesn't mean we aren't impacted.

Becoming tender with the wounds of our trauma is a journey, one Joseph's life beautifully depicts. To be made tender is to find a level of comfort in the thin spaces of our grief.

What's fascinating about the story of Joseph is the author doesn't mention Joseph weeping until *after* his life begins to look better. The text doesn't say he weeps when his brothers' envy pushes them to throw their own blood into a pit (though he does display emotion). He doesn't cry when he is sold into slavery and given to Potiphar. He doesn't cry when, after being freed, he is falsely accused and thrown *back* into prison. He doesn't cry when he is forgotten by Pharaoh's cupbearer. Through the anger, the uncertainty, and the betrayal, we do not bear witness to Joseph being moved to tears. The author is very intentional when speaking of the times that Joseph weeps.

Joseph suffers with dry eyes, but he remembers with tears.

The first time we see Joseph cry is in Genesis 42. By this time Joseph has endured a life of slavery under Potiphar after being sold by his own flesh and blood and has spent years in prison despite his innocence. After interpreting several dreams and proving his character to Pharaoh, Joseph is promoted and becomes one of his officials. During this time, a famine depletes his homeland, and his brothers come to Egypt to get food for their family. They do not recognize Joseph, but he recognizes them. They have come to Egypt desperate for a rescue. There, in front of Joseph, they confess that their struggle is because of what they have done in the past, unaware of who they are speaking to.

> They said to one another, "Surely we are being punished because of our brother. We saw how distressed he was when he pleaded with us for his life, but we would not listen; that's why this distress has come on us." (Gen. 42:21 NIV)

How audacious. For Joseph, the actions of his brothers had catapulted him into a life of profound anguish and suffering. And here they are, discussing their regret over what was done, not because they are convicted of the evil of their actions but because they fear they are experiencing some kind of karma.

Even though all these events set the stage for God's redemption further in the story, in that moment it doesn't matter that Joseph finally has the upper hand. It doesn't matter that his experiences have been redeemed in his favor. Or that he is no longer a slave and is in a position of power. None of that keeps the tears at bay—because memories have a way of breaking our hearts a second time. So Joseph "turned away from them and began to weep" (v. 24 NIV).

Many times, our memories of pain can harden us in the same way the original wounds can. But from what we read about Joseph and all he goes through, it's safe to conclude that his heart remains soft toward the Lord. It is soft enough to find a way to serve others with his gift while he is bound and in prison—and has every reason to withhold his help out of bitterness. It is soft enough to flee from temptation when he is seduced and to forfeit the chance to tell his side of the story (39:12–18).

We present Joseph as the hero of the story because he trusts God and forgives his brothers. But the story of Joseph illustrates the power of our Divine Hero entering both our trauma and the stories we tell ourselves.

I see Joseph in those of you who may struggle with the belief that your trauma has robbed you of the ability to stay soft. Joseph has done the work of trusting God in the pit and in prison. But as he sits in a position of power, despite the proof that God came to his rescue and restored his life, there is still a wound.

You may have come out of the valley unscathed by the temptation to let disappointment, cynicism, and fear packaged as self-righteousness harden your heart. But there is still the aftermath, the wound, the memories, and the story. Sometimes we desperately want God to make us soft by making the pain from what happened to us disappear. But some things stick to us, even when circumstances are better.

God can make us tender through the tears we shed when the residue of the things we survived shows up even in better times.

If you are like me, you want the miracle of becoming soft to be instantaneous. But life ebbs and flows in such a way that there will always be this rhythm of being hardened and returning to tenderness. In Genesis 42, for all he has endured, Joseph seemingly comes out on top with his heart intact, and yet he weeps in a way that reveals corners of his heart that still need softening. For Joseph, as for all of us, becoming soft is a process God is continually working within us.

There are times when we are softened not by confessing our sins but by letting God touch what we painfully remember. And memory is such a curious thing. We tend to recall what we want to forget and forget what we wish we could remember. But I've cried enough tears to fill a pool—enough to know tears make us tender. God does not make us tender by rushing us to a place of resolution where we are ok with what happened to us. Rather, our tears can lead us to a healed and restored heart by way of lamenting.

Lament and grief are sisters. When we grieve, we are swept up by the tide of loss, overcome by the force of losing someone or something. Lamenting empowers us to recall God's faithfulness as we reckon with a life riddled with loss. There is a softening when we grieve the love we never received, the words we never heard, and the safety we weren't afforded. The tears make us tender because they validate our pain and everything we've been through, and it is in this painful remembrance that God meets us to tell us we are seen and loved through it all.

Joseph carried years and moments of pain, and the Scripture never makes mention of tears. Not until he comes face-to-face with his brothers. Not until the grief that was living in his bones begins to sing. And so Joseph weeps. Joseph grieves. He grieves how his brothers love Benjamin in a way they never loved him (44:18–45:2).

The most heartbreaking scene is when Joseph finally reveals himself to his brothers, proclaiming, "It's me! The one you hurt, the one you discarded! It's me, your brother whom you treated as anything but." Genesis 45:2 says that when Joseph finally reveals his identity to his brothers, he sobs so loud that the Egyptian attendants he told to leave the room could hear him. I can relate to that ache.

When we are offered the blessing of mourning, we are wise to receive it, as Joseph does. We can let our tears become our lament of all the wrongs we have endured, even and especially if we've downplayed them in the past or worked hard to put them behind us. Joseph weeps a total of seven times. Some tears he sheds for his own pain, some for his loss, and some for others. Joseph's sensitivity is anything but a curse. In fact, it's a blessing. The tears he sheds lead him to the tender moment we see in Genesis 50.

Joseph returns to Egypt with his brothers after burying their father. As his brothers settle into their new home, they fear that Joseph's kindness will fade and he will do to them what they did to him. They decide to appease Joseph by using his fondness for their late father, Jacob. They send a message claiming that Jacob asked Joseph to forgive his brothers of his sins. Joseph responds with tears. When the brothers arrive in person, they fall before him and declare themselves his slaves.

Joseph has every right to respond with vengeance. They deserve to be treated in the same way they'd treated him.

But the weeping has done its work on Joseph's heart. His mourning has blessed him with a revelation. Joseph says to his brothers, "Don't be afraid. Am I in the place of God? You intended to harm me, but God intended it for good to accomplish what is now being done, the saving of many lives" (50:19–20 NIV). Joseph's tears allow him to change the story he's been telling himself. His mourning blesses him with the glory of a new story.

To come face-to-face with the stories we tell ourselves is not easy. And yet it's in grieving what was and what never could be that we shed the tears that shed the armor off our hearts. I remember where I was when I screamed to the heavens with receipts that the story I had been telling myself was in fact true: "Girls like me don't get good things, God!" I'd been wounded toward the lie that God could not touch the jagged edges that were left in the dark.

Dancing with a Limp

I used to puff up whenever someone commented on my ability to stay soft. I would nod my head with a sense of unwarranted pride, as if this miracle was the proof of my own diligence. And while there is an aspect of guarding our hearts, the ability to be made tender despite the trauma we endure is miraculous.

We've all experienced the kind of trauma that lingers underneath ordinary moments and makes it hard to imagine life free from the weight of our triggers. But God is in the work of gently walking us along the path marked tender as we stumble and find our bearings. He is patient as we crawl and as we are hesitant to trust that we are not too much for God.

Writer Anne Lamott speaks of grief as coming through something with a "leg that never heals perfectly—that still hurts when the weather is cold—but you learn to dance with the limp."[3] When the enemy of our souls mocks our triggers as evidence that God will not touch our grief, we can be confident that we are still becoming whole—and God is always with us.

And we learn to dance with a limp. To continue to heal. To let the tears fall honestly. To face the stories we tell ourselves again and again. To find the courage to hand over the pen.

I still carry the story written that night I pulled my mom back into the car. I still have instances in life when that little girl appears and tells me, *Girls like you don't get good things.* However, she's no longer the remnant of what can never be but rather a reminder of how God is still softening the woman who survived.

Being made soft doesn't look like God erasing the memory of what we've been through. And the weeping that still endures in the night doesn't mean we don't still carry a heart tender toward the Lord. We choose to be brave enough to waltz with our wounds. To exchange the stories they told for the ones God writes on our journey of being made tender.

We learn to twirl with hope that our trauma is not too much for God's hand to make tender. We dance with our therapists, with our friends, with our Lord—with those who understand that our limp is just proof of our need and desire to be made whole. Our limp reminds us that no trauma can rob us of a soft heart.

7

THE TREE REMEMBERS

*The Nature of True Forgiveness
That Actually Frees Us to Heal*

Forgive and forget. Forgive and forget. Forgive and forget. I mentally recited the words as the water ran through my fingers while I washed up from dinner. It had been almost a year since the day my whole world flipped upside down. This moment foreshadowed the kind of mental gymnastics I would perform for the next three years to gather a sense of peace. I grew up being taught that forgiveness was the default response as a mature person of faith. Forgiveness was the expectation after an offense. It was what you did as a "good Christian." It was my duty, but rarely my delight. The way I saw it, forgiveness was an obligation, but it never felt like true ointment for the gash. It was simply what had to be done. As I repeated *forgive and forget* to myself, I stared out the window at my son playing in the backyard, and my chest began to burn with anger. In that moment, forgiveness didn't seem like enough. It wasn't enough to keep my indignation from boiling up my throat or hot tears from streaming down my face.

Forgiveness was supposed to be the magic trick of my faith. It was supposed to be the final step to moving forward. The proof that I was not a "pretend believer" but a woman after God's own heart. The evidence that I belonged to God and not to my pain. The act of closing the case on the past offense.

But it wasn't. I began to treat forgiveness like a big red "easy" button with the word *forgive* painted on it in white. Year after year, offense after offense, betrayal after betrayal, I hit the button, which was easier to do as a trained impulse than to deal with the difficult emotions true forgiveness raises. There were times when I would withhold it for months, not ready to offer what I didn't feel, but ultimately I'd hit the button again and just get it over with.

Sometimes we are more desperate to stop hurting than to start the journey of healing. We would rather hit the button than find ourselves at the feet of Jesus wrestling with this commandment that feels like a mockery of our pain. We don't want to shed the tears that come with the confession that we feel God couldn't possibly know the depth of our hurt.

We gird ourselves with this perfunctory form of forgiveness. The type that's done out of "holy" obligation but lacks the power to mend the stab wounds of our hearts. We slap the easy button and practice forgiveness as a one-time event instead of a lifetime journey.

We carry on with this false expression of forgiveness, eyeing the stockpile of all the hurts hidden under the rug in the middle of the living room of our hearts. Adding to it when we are triggered, when we remember what was done, when we consider how the other person isn't truly sorry. And because we are operating with a manufactured forgiveness that hasn't been touched by the power of God, we do not soften when we respond to another person's apology (or absence thereof). Instead, we playact forgiveness as a shortcut, skirting the in-depth, whole-person, messy process it requires.

True forgiveness is balm for our wounded souls. Jesus is clear that the healing power forgiveness carries doesn't come from our will and determination to muster up the phrases we believe prove our maturity. The healing power of the type of forgiveness God calls us to is from Him alone.

The mystery and wonder of forgiveness—both offered to us and flowing from us—is what liberates us to be both soft and strong. Forgiveness is the journey we walk to be made soft.

Mustard Seeds of Faith

I didn't grow up spending much time with my grandmother. I knew of her but didn't know much about her. She would send me cards filled with her cursive script saying, "Happy Birthday," and giving me a blessing. That was the extent of our interaction until adulthood.

So it was no surprise that I stumbled over my words when I picked up the phone to ask if the kids and I could stay with her while we moved back to Colorado for the final time. I half-heartedly expected her to say no and let out a sigh of relief when she offered me a matter-of-fact yes, as if my question held a foregone conclusion. That was just my grandmother.

She was never the nurturing kind. I don't remember being swallowed up by her hugs growing up. But what she lacked in warmth she possessed in wisdom.

I wasn't at my grandmother's house for long. But I was there long enough to understand that I was living in the legacy of her faith. I would hear her humming hymns as she scooted around the kitchen in her wheelchair. Every evening, after putting the kids down, I'd climb up the stairs to find her watching the news, sighing and shaking her head at the state of the world. And almost every night she would whisper the same thing: "Forgive them, Father."

It didn't come as a shock to me, then, when her only advice to me in the middle of my sea of suffering was to forgive the father of my children. "It's the only way to be free," she said, with her eyes glued to her crossword puzzle. I smiled and whispered, "I know, Grandma, I know," before heading back downstairs, determined to avoid any more lectures. But my grandma never brought it up again. There was no need for repetition because what she said while she scribbled into her crossword was what she meant. Forgiveness was simple—it was that simple. Or maybe it was so sacred that, in her devotion to God, it had become *that* simple for her. She had lived her life extending forgiveness that didn't need an explanation. Forgiveness that stood on Calvary, not on her own might.

I struggled with the ease in which she called me to the same resolve. To me, forgiveness felt anything but simple.

After bearing the brunt of pain at the hands of another, we squirm at forgiveness because we believe it calls us to immediately bear a burden that will make us look and feel weak. But that is, in fact, the point. The journey of forgiveness makes us fully aware of our weaknesses, yes—and also fully strengthens us by God's arrival of grace for us on the very same road. A forgiveness that *feels* powerful will leave us wanting. A forgiveness detached from a humble understanding both of our own shortcomings and that we are covered with mercy does not leave us softer. Instead it causes us to cover our own iniquities with reason while demanding those who offend us are laid bare in the courtroom of our vindication.

And yet, even knowing this, we can still find ourselves at a crossroads, staring down the path of forgiveness and vowing to never walk it again. I couldn't forgive the man I still loved but no longer trusted and no longer viewed the same. Oh, I could say the words. I *had* said the words, but only out of sheer desperation that their utterance would be an easy-button remedy. I detached them from any true intention to walk the journey of time and healing or reckon with what obedience would require of me.

If it were up to me, true forgiveness would not be possible. If it were up to me, he didn't deserve my forgiveness in the same way he believed I didn't deserve an apology. If it were up to me, withholding forgiveness was the only card I had left to play, the only remnant of power I had left. It was the only thing I could leverage to stop feeling weak.

If it were up to us, we'd be content (superficially) to live void of the very freedom we need most, thinking it enough to demand we get what we believe we are owed. If it were up to us, we'd opt out of forgiveness altogether in the belief that it would produce in us a weakness to be exploited. If it were up to us, we would take the partial healing that comes without forgiveness and pretend to be satisfied.

But true forgiveness isn't bound by our ability. It may begin with our will to say yes, but it's not sustained by our might.

Try as we may, we cannot manufacture the miracle of walking in forgiveness. When we consider the power of God, we might think pillars of cloud and fire, seas and rivers parting, or a divine display of intervention. We rarely consider *forgiveness* as the manifestation of His full power amid His people. And yet that's exactly what forgiveness is: God's power on display.

In Luke 17, Jesus teaches the disciples on forgiveness, acknowledging an impossibility—but it's not the one we would identify. "Offenses will certainly come" (v. 1 CSB). Christ says it openly: the hurt is bound to happen. In this life, we will always experience something that needs to be forgiven. And to follow Him requires we place our feet on the path of forgiveness—one filled with many pit stops that beckon us to forgive yet again. Jesus continues, revealing the habitual nature of forgiveness: "Even if they sin against you seven times in a day and seven times come back to you saying 'I repent,' you must forgive them" (v. 4 NIV).

The disciples realize that forgiving according to Christ's standard is impossible in their own efforts. They cry out, "Increase our faith" (v. 5).

Society presents forgiveness as an act of sheer will—a decision we come to when and if we feel the desire to do so. Within this view, forgiveness is an option—the weaker option. The better option is withholding forgiveness when it's felt to be undeserved, as an act of agency and power.

But it's clear here in this verse, and in many others where God speaks of forgiveness, that it is not optional. To forgive is to obey what God has asked of us. Obedience is always tethered to our faith—faith in who God says He is and in what He promises to do with the yes that we offer.

It's a hard pill to swallow. But it's a pill that goes down with the waters of trust.

We grow hard toward God because we try to will ourselves to do what we cannot do on our own. Our hearts harden when we try to take on in our own strength what is only possible with God. And when it doesn't "work"—when we struggle to step forward on the path laden with "I forgive you seventy times seven"—we decide what's being asked of us is a cruel and unachievable task.

We've all asked ourselves these questions:

How could God expect me to forgive the unforgivable?

Where is the goodness in extending mercy when it will only have to be extended again?

Did God not see me stuck in the snare?

Did He not bear witness to the injuries I sustained?

Most of us know what God has to say about forgiveness. We know that much of Scripture is filled with Christ telling us to forgive. But our inability to forgive in our own strength can lead us to considering that what was said wasn't meant. The healing that comes with true forgiveness isn't meant for us, we think, because we are too hurt. The offense was too great. There was no apology. And so we dethrone God in our hearts and conclude that God has no business asking us to forgive.

This was the disciples' honest reaction when they heard Jesus's radical call to forgiveness. And this was Jesus's response:

"And if he sins against you seven times in a day, and comes back to you seven times, saying, 'I repent,' you must forgive him."
The apostles said to the Lord, "Increase our faith."

"If you have the faith the size of a mustard seed," the Lord said, *"you can say to this mulberry tree, 'Be uprooted and planted in the sea,' and it will obey you."* (Luke 17:4–6)

The disciples are reeling with the *how* of this seemingly impossible ask, and Jesus quickly assures them that all they need is the smallest measure of faith imaginable. Faith the size of a mustard seed is all we need for the miracle of forgiveness to take place in our hearts.

Here we see a hard command paired with tremendous grace. The type of grace that gives us the bravery to not just hear what Jesus said but believe it's what He meant—and respond accordingly. Our will to forgive is empowered by God's will to *help* us forgive. What our might alone cannot cover, true forgiveness that leans on faith can redeem.

We are made soft through forgiveness because it is the fruit of our faith, not of our willpower. And the revelation of the flow of forgiveness toward us keeps our hearts tender when God asks the same forgiveness to flow from us.

As He Forgives, We Can Forgive

I spent so much time, in my effort to forgive, looking at who hurt me. My focus was on "them" understanding the weight of the harm they'd done. I was obsessed with my desire for them to feel my pain and consumed with a need to see them figuratively (and frankly, literally) fall to their knees as the revelation of the harm they caused finally hit them.

One evening I was at a worship night at my church when I had a very intimate conversation with God in the middle of the crowded sanctuary. I sat as the band played, and my mind found itself ruminating on my desire for those who hurt me to feel pain. And then a question dropped in my heart: *What about Me?*

I heard the words from the depths of my spirit and knew they weren't my own. *What do You mean, God?* I thought.

What about Me, Charaia? What about Me can move you toward forgiveness?

I didn't understand. Until I did.

I had lost sight of Him. Somewhere along the way forgiveness had become conditional to me—it could only be extended if the person who hurt me understood their need for my forgiveness, understood the pain they caused me, or begged me for mercy. My obedience was held hostage by their willingness to apologize.

In Ephesians, we're instructed to forgive *just as* Christ forgave us (4:32). In Colossians, Paul encourages believers to bear with one another and to forgive *as the Lord* forgives (3:13). Authentic forgiveness will always be our response when we consider the extravagant grace we receive.

Ultimately, how we forgive is an illustration of how we believe Christ forgives us.

When it comes to forgiving *as Christ*, many of us have distanced ourselves from the revelation that we are constantly living in the streams of His mercy. And when we lack this revelation, we resist. We then rage at the thought of God covering someone who doesn't deserve it and resist what's for our own good. When we've become desensitized to our own iniquity, we're emboldened to deem our transgressions as minor and others' as monuments too big to be pardoned. And so we withhold the very mercy we receive ourselves and call God cruel for asking us to extend it.

In so many ways, we've watered down, belittled, and boxed up the forgiveness of God. It's known but not believed. *Can God truly forgive the things that only He bore witness to? Can He truly forgive the secret acts I could not afford for the world to discover? Does God really forgive me over and over? Have I reached God's forgiveness quota for the week, the month, the year?* We aren't persuaded that God does in fact cover a multitude of sins. We struggle to believe He is good when He asks us to extend mercy, just as He is good in His extension of mercy.

True forgiveness is the overflow of the divine forgiveness given to us. This is why Christ does not tell us to forgive as we *feel* or forgive as we deem fit but to forgive *as He forgave us*. Because the truth is that a revelation of God's forgiveness toward us will always provoke the desire to be more forgiving.

What Forgiveness Is Not

Having a poor theology of forgiveness weakens our desire to forgive as we are forgiven. We must confront what forgiveness is not in order to stay in the fight to be made tender through forgiveness. The story of my marriage coming to an end is filled with my misunderstanding of true forgiveness, repentance, and reconciliation. But I remember the moment when some of the myths of forgiveness were broken.

My husband had returned from his deployment only for me to discover the mistake he'd made in tech school had happened again. I sat in the rattan chair in the corner of my room while my daughter nursed before bed. I could feel rage bubbling up in my throat. I had been here before, and if I followed the same cycle again, I would rush through the stages of rage and grief to get to the "easy button" kind of forgiveness that was by now so familiar to me. But as I stared at him sitting across the room, I knew what I needed to do. I couldn't stay.

"I'm leaving," I whispered to him. My tone was defeated and tired. I didn't have a plan or a place, but I knew that to force myself to forgive and reconcile in the same beat would be the death of me. I knew it would harden my heart. Something had to change.

"I'm leaving." I repeated the phrase, this time to myself.

I wasn't surprised by my husband's shock. He was used to me doing what I'd always done: forgive and forget in a way that meant moving on without healing. Not even a year prior to this confession in my bedroom, I had forgiven him faster than I could grieve the trust that had died. And it took months for me to realize that my understanding of forgiveness was deeply incomplete, in that I believed forgiveness always went hand in hand with reconciliation. How wrong I was.

That belief had led to a betrayal of my own self. Many of us withhold forgiveness because we know we can't afford to betray our own sense of safety and justice by letting the one who hurt us back into our lives. We've been taught forgiveness and reconciliation within the same message—but Jesus never taught this. God never forces us to let people who have hurt us unrepentantly back into our lives.

For me, I did not know what the evidence of repentance was. Many of us are stalled in our healing because we have never been taught that true forgiveness does not require reconciliation.

Reconciliation is one gift of forgiveness, but it is not the only gift. Sometimes the gift is walking away from a toxic relationship and into our freedom—without looking back. I need you to know that God's commands will never lead us to a place of harm. Forgiveness is the heart of the Father, but reconciliation without repentance is not.

That day, I drew a line in the sand. It was a hard no that I wished could be different. But we can only make choices for ourselves, no matter how much we wish those who have hurt us would choose differently.

As Paul writes, sorrow over one's actions is a start, but it must be followed by the fruit of true repentance, which he describes as a process:

> Consider what this godly sorrow has produced in you: what earnestness, what eagerness to clear yourselves, what indignation, what alarm, what longing, what zeal, what vindication! In every way you have proved yourselves to be innocent in this matter. So even though I wrote to you, it was not on account of the one who did wrong or the one who was harmed, but rather that your earnestness on our behalf would be made clear to you in the sight of God. On account of this, we are encouraged. (2 Cor. 7:11–13 BSB)

Repentance is the prerequisite for reconciliation. Any teaching that pressures us to reconnect without first witnessing the fruit of repentance is not a biblical understanding of forgiveness. It's cheap atonement that burdens the wounded and enables the behavior of the offender. Second Corinthians lays out what repentance looks like. When we are hurt and make the decision to forgive, we have done all that we can do without the other person. But reconciliation requires a willingness from the offender to let repentance be produced in them. This teaching from Paul is important for our protection through our discernment in environments where there is harm. It is easy to betray ourselves, for the sake of reconciliation, by choosing not to commit to bear witness to repentance before remaining in relationship.

Godly sorrow is not just the emotion of feeling bad. It's the experience of having a heart grieved by what has been done—and taking personal responsibility for it. And then wading through that grief with an eagerness to clear ourselves. Paul makes clear that true repentance is "not on account of the one who did wrong or the one who was harmed" (v. 12 BSB). We do not change in a meaningful way by considering ourselves or even the one we hurt. Repentance that reforms our behavior is done when we consider *Christ*. It's our desire to reconcile with Christ that produces a desire to reconcile with others.

In our yearning to fix what was broken by the brokenness of someone we love, we can silence our discernment in favor of our desire to reconnect. If we do, after a while we'll grow weary in our attempt to either see what is not there (the fruit of repentance) or accept what will never be.

Real reconciliation is not the act of accepting toxic behavior to avoid fracturing a relationship. It's the marriage of two decisions: yours for forgiveness and theirs for repentance, intertwined with one another.

When I chose to make the decision to draw a line in the context of my marriage, I was terrified. Before that, in some way, I had been hoping that my extension of forgiveness would inspire my husband to change. But the truth is that change and true repentance are inspired by the Holy Spirit.

The other person's desire to be in right relationship with God is what matters, not any of our attempts to get them to change simply because we forgive them.

Forgiveness is not synonymous with reconciliation. The relational repair we hope for may or may not ever happen. Yet while another's choice for repentance is their own to make, we can make our choice to forgive and walk free no matter what they do. And sometimes the boundaries we set are ways we can protect the heart God made soft when we made the decision to forgive. There will be times when we must put up a fence that's stained with our own tears to keep our hearts tender to what God wants to do with our yes.

Another misconception that can keep us from receiving the freedom of forgiveness is this belief that we are to "forgive and forget." The Shona people of Zimbabwe have a proverb that says "the ax forgets, but the tree remembers." Forgiveness is a journey, and much of the theology surrounding forgiveness lacks this truth. We bind ourselves to this false belief that we have not forgiven if we remember. But the path of forgiveness is filled with steps that all look the same and are filled with memories the ax likely doesn't recall. The path calls us to whisper, "I forgive and I release," as often as we recall.

That is forgiveness.

It's a miracle that meets us as we remember how we've been hurt but also how we have received mercy upon mercy from God. It's a commandment that doesn't require amnesia but rather another mustard seed of faith, planted in the ground and watered with our tears. It's the doing again and again as we remember what Christ has done for us. The tree never forgets the way the ax sliced it. It never forgets the pain it felt as its trunk was cut. We rarely remember the ways we hurt others in the same way we recall how we've been hurt. And in a way, remembering protects us just as forgiving frees us. So as you remember, may you forgive—until one day, the memory will cross your mind and not your heart. It will be thought and not felt. One day you will recall without recoiling, and that is the reward of walking the path of forgiveness and letting it make you tender.

An Invitation to the Journey

Out of all the chapters in this book, this was the hardest to write. Not because I don't believe in the words I've written but because I'm well acquainted with how hard forgiveness can be. I know what it's like to sit at the feet of Jesus in anguish over what He is asking as I pursue the healing that comes on the other side of forgiveness.

Just as forgiveness is not a magic trick that can make the pain of an offense vanish, my words won't magically make you forgive. But what I can offer is sympathy, and in case you haven't heard it, I am sorry. I am sorry they hurt you. I am sorry they betrayed you. I am sorry they mishandled you. I am sorry they abused you. I am sorry you're still waiting on an apology or acknowledgment. I am sorry their actions didn't match their words.

Here is my invitation for you to start the courageous journey of true forgiveness. To enter into the spiritual practice of releasing judgment of another's wrongs to God, and therefore releasing yourself from resentment, bitterness, and rage. True forgiveness is the active choice of letting go of vengeance and letting God be the one to deal with those who have harmed you. It is the active choice of recognizing the hurt while letting God be the one to both condemn the wrong and make right. And the good news is that on the cross, Christ fulfilled His own commandment. He doesn't just arbitrarily demand we walk the hard path of forgiveness; He stepped onto it first Himself.

This is why we can find Him trustworthy. He doesn't call us to places He has not traveled. He doesn't lead us to roads that aren't marked with His own footprints. Jesus put on flesh not just to redeem humanity but to sympathize with us in our own.

The very good truth is that forgiving is for *us*. It gives us a chance to center Christ in our story and not the harm. It grants us freedom that is not held hostage by someone's apology.

My hope is that you are first softened by the promise that the path of forgiveness is not one you are expected to walk alone. My hope is that you would accept forgiveness as an active path and not a potion you drink to feel better about the past. It is the path to peace and the radical acceptance that the past couldn't be any different.

My hope is that you would believe you are worthy of a life where you don't have to keep tripping over the handle of the ax you half-buried and called forgiven. More than anything, I hope that you believe now, more than before, that to forgive is not to accept what was done. It is not to remain with unrepentant people for the sake of proving that you are able to forgive.

My hope is that you would receive the miracle of freedom that comes from releasing the things you cannot forget, the hurt you did not deserve, and the apology you may never receive. Your healing is worth your own fight to forgive. And the God of forgiveness Himself fights for you all the way.

8

THE JOB EQUATION

The Miracle of Getting through
Suffering with a Soft Heart

I woke up in a sweat. It had been a couple of weeks since I'd relocated to my father's home in Colorado after making the hard decision to enter a season of separation with my husband. After he returned from a six-month deployment in the middle of the pandemic, a joyous homecoming quickly turned into heartbreak. I think back to the day I called my dad. I dialed his number as the only person I knew who could offer me a sense of refuge. I whispered, "Dad, I need to come home," trying not to let the word *home* get stuck in my throat. Within a few days, my dad took a flight to Georgia, drove four hours to the town I was in, and was on my doorstep.

I sat up in the dark and cold room as these memories filled my mind. The adrenaline of making the quick decision to separate was wearing off, and I was crumbling. I slid away from acting as my two-month-old daughter's pillow and tip-toed to the bathroom. The mirror was full of sticky notes with Scriptures reminding me it would all be ok.

But it wasn't ok.

I wasn't ok.

It wasn't supposed to be like this. I wasn't supposed to be here, in my father's bathroom, sharing a room with both my children because my marriage was hanging by a thread. I gripped the edge of the counter and let out a quiet groan that held the grief of the past two years. The betrayal, the loneliness, the fear, the heartbreak, the pain. Lifting my head to meet my reflection, I wept because I didn't recognize myself. I knew suffering was promised. I knew how to spin my hurt into an object lesson for a blog post or social media caption. And yet I didn't know how to preserve my softness when I was in survival mode. I didn't know how to stop living with my breath held and my jaw clenched, anticipating the next blow.

The suffering was starting to stick.

I could accept the road to developing character, at least for a time. I was fine with suffering if I could feel its expiration approaching. I was prepared to suffer so long as it didn't push me too far from how things were supposed to be. But by now it all felt too far. I had suffered longer than I wanted to—longer than I felt I should have or deserved to. I was suffering burns from the flames of fires I never ignited. If I was honest, it hadn't automatically led me to a "but God" moment. I had to fight for that proclamation, and I wasn't there yet.

We're so quick to present the theology of suffering as the means to an end. And we define "the end" as the moment we deem our suffering has lasted long enough to produce a reward. A reward we want to hold in our living, mortal hands. Abraham suffered until he didn't—and was given a son. Hannah suffered until she didn't—and conceived a son. Job suffered until he didn't—and everything was restored back to him. We tend to bypass the middle space where these characters in the Bible held their pain toward the promise. We'd rather preach a form of suffering that only produces our own glory story.

Yet Christ makes it clear that there is no glory without the suffering of the cross.

Looking back at my own seasons of strife, I can see there was a form of comfort I created by wrapping my being in the clothes of my hurt. I moved from being a victim of the broken things of the world to playing victim as if I were cast in life to play such a role—to show up to every scene waiting for the opportunity to list all the ways in which I had been hurt and still was hurt. I teetered on the line of vulnerability and figuratively bled on anyone who got close enough to soak up a droplet. But behind both the obsession and avoidance of suffering is a desire to be seen. We long for someone to bear witness to what we've been through.

Suffering alone doesn't case our hearts with layers of protection. In fact, the Scriptures make it clear that enduring suffering produces the type of heart able to see Jesus in affliction. God has been clear that pain is part of the human experience. And though we know this, there's a resistance to the truth that, as believers, we are *promised* suffering. Somewhere along the way, we hear this truth but decide we can spend much of our lives expecting God to break His promise. We consider ourselves the great exception to this human rule—*surely the worst happens to other people, but not to us!*

Underneath this resistance to pain is a belief that humankind is the center of the story. The tension to suffer for the sake of His name crushes us on either side because we don't believe Christ is truly worth it. We think He's only worth the type of suffering that has a time stamp, that doesn't leave us wounded—that doesn't plunge us toward complete dependence on Him.

If we were being candid, many of us would confess that the God we've created in our own image is not worth the suffering He calls us to.

But there is a hope that a soft heart can be preserved through suffering. And it begins with a refusal to reduce suffering to a means to an end and an embrace of suffering as the place where we encounter the God who makes us tender.

The Job Equation

Of all the stories in the Bible, Job's has always been presented as a tale of restoration and not one of great suffering. For me, at least, the book of Job was presented as a quite simple journey of a man who lost it all, believed God through it all, and got it all back. I came to resent the way many have used this text to reduce suffering to what I call the "Job equation."

The equation goes like this: *If I am a good Christian, when I suffer, my fortunes will be doubly restored.* Such a very Westernized retelling of Job promises that the sole purpose of suffering is to watch God restore. And while I'm not here to paint a pessimistic picture of the ways in which the kingdom operates, it does the body of Christ no good to refuse to tell the whole truth of suffering. When we refuse to accept that suffering is endured to encounter more of Christ, we will find ourselves hardened by hardship. When we view suffering as simply our ticket to being "paid back" in material rewards, we will find ourselves vastly disillusioned when it turns out to be a process of stripping the parts of us that want to be like God: in charge.

A closer look at Job's story reveals the equation gets it all wrong. Job is one of a trilogy of wisdom books in the Bible that also includes Proverbs and Ecclesiastes. In Proverbs we learn that God rewards the righteous and punishes the wicked. Yet the writer of Ecclesiastes concludes that life is not fair and is rather like a mist that cannot be explained or even understood. We leave Ecclesiastes wondering, *If life is unfair to the righteous, then is God fair and just?* The book of Job uses Job's life to work this question out. How can a just God watch those He loves wither under the weight of suffering? How can a good God allow Satan to strip a righteous man of everything he has? When we attempt to box the story of Job into a lesson of pushing through pain for our reward, we miss the wisdom laced within the layers of Job's suffering.

Let's take a look at where this story begins, so that we might better understand its depths.

One day the sons of God came to present themselves before the LORD, and Satan also came with them. The LORD asked Satan, "Where have you come from?"

"From roaming through the earth," Satan answered him, "and walking around on it."

Then the LORD said to Satan, "Have you considered my servant Job? No one else on earth is like him, a man of perfect integrity, who fears God and turns away from evil."

Satan answered the LORD, "Does Job fear God for nothing? Haven't you placed a hedge around him, his household, and everything he owns? You have blessed the work of his hands, and his possessions have increased in the land. But stretch out your hand and strike everything he owns, and he will surely curse you to your face."

"Very well," the LORD told Satan, "everything he owns is in your power." (Job 1:6–12)

Satan approaches the Lord that day in the heavens with a bold accusation. After God boasts of Job's integrity and character, Satan responds with his claim that Job was only obedient to God because of the favor on his life. If God were to remove the hedge of protection surrounding Job and allow affliction to bear down on him, his affection would change.

Job then loses everything in a way familiar to many of us: in wave after wave. A messenger comes to tell Job that his oxen and donkeys have been stolen, and the servants looking after them were also killed (1:14–15). "While he was still speaking," a second messenger tells Job that a fire has burned up his sheep and his servants with them (v. 16 NIV). "While he was still speaking," a third messenger tells Job that his camels have been stolen and still more of his servants killed (v. 17 NIV). "While he was still speaking," yet another messenger comes and lets him know that a "mighty wind" has caused the house filled with his sons and daughters to collapse—crushing and killing them all (vv. 18–19 NIV).

Devastation after devastation. Job finds himself on a hamster wheel of suffering where it's never simply one thing at a time but everything all at once. And yet Job, like us, in the beginning of suffering when the hope that God will bring an end to our pain is still close enough to grasp, still praises God in the middle of the rubble.

> Then Job stood up, tore his robe, and shaved his head. He fell to the ground and worshiped, saying:
>
>> Naked I came from my mother's womb,
>> and naked I will leave this life.
>> The LORD gives, and the LORD takes away.
>> Blessed be the name of the LORD. (vv. 20–21)

In the wake of great loss, Job preserves his soft heart by covering his suffering with what he knows to be true of the Lord. Likewise, since we know suffering is promised, while it knocks the wind out of us, it doesn't *always* knock out our willingness to see God in it. Not at first—so long as we believe we're still operating within the Job equation of suffering.

Satan goes on to attack Job a second time. He's sure he will crush Job until he curses God. But when Job's own wife tells him to curse God after she bears witness to the devastation, he refuses. Instead, he asks her, "Should we accept only good from God and not adversity?" (2:10). It's an honorable response that initially made me question if Job was even human. And I suppose that is the point—to show us what is produced when our humanity is completely devoted to His divinity. The pain produces praise.

This is where a lot of the teaching surrounding Job jumps to the end of the story. We paint Job with brushes dipped in a theology of suffering that doesn't last long and always leads to the glory of a happy ending. We reduce the forty-two-chapter book into a tale of riches to rags to riches, because we're prone to despise the suffering that calls us out of our own understanding. But when we do so, we cheat ourselves of the witness being laid out for us: we do not know exactly how long Job sat in the ashes, but we can confidently conclude it was longer than he wanted.

We miss the depth of the text when we don't recognize the boils that covered Job's skin are the same boils that covered his people's oppressors in Egypt and those who were disobedient (Deut. 28:27). And we miss it when we don't consider how this would leave a righteous man like Job feeling cursed by God.

When we erase the Job equation from our reading, from our understanding of Job, we can see that we only intensify the anguish of the valley when we focus on the ending—and not on the God waiting to be found in the journey.

When I removed the equation, I realized I don't suffer like Job. I'd guess that is true for many of us. Walking through suffering without wrestling with how our pain makes us feel about God only strips our hearts of softness. Laying our genuine ache at the altar is what keeps us soft in our affliction.

Adversity can crack our hearts. But the impact of affliction doesn't damage the heart as much as the prolonged nature of hardship does. In the middle of a storm we are less tempted to question God's goodness or allow our tribulation to inform what we believe to be true about His character when we can still catch a glimpse of the shoreline.

It's the suffering that feels never-ending that hardens our hearts. The suffering that causes us to say, "He doesn't let me catch my breath but fills me with bitter experiences" (9:18). It's the beliefs we form in the wreckage that rob us of the ability to remain tender through the pain.

The Conclusions We Come To

If I am suffering, God must not be what I once believed. If I am suffering, God must not be good. If I am suffering, God must not be just. And if all this is true, God is not trustworthy to hold my heart through affliction.

I wrote these words in my journal after coming under yet another wave in my season of suffering. My journal was filled with questions and statements revealing what I truly thought of God. We think affliction reveals the truth of God. That even though we were taught He is good, our suffering reveals He is not. Where we thought He is just, our suffering reveals He is not. But what adversity reveals is not the truth of God but what we consider to be true about God. Belief, not sentiment, comes to the surface in the same way literal and figurative boils come to the surface of our being.

How we speak of God when we are suffering matters. The conclusions we let our wounds draw amid our pain can affect the map that leads us through suffering softly—with our hearts still open to the goodness of God, even when we are in pain.

What keeps us from getting to the other side of affliction with a soft heart intact is a redefinition of God's character. When we let our wounds whisper the "truth" about who God is, and when we begin to doubt His unwavering love for us, that is when the heart begins to harden. It's a fully human response.

And yet, it's not the only conclusion we can make. Rather, God invites us to be honest with Him about our hurt, to honor where He is at work in our story, and to pour our hearts out to Him in the midst of our suffering. He is a God who can handle it—as Scripture's many laments show us again and again. Of all the truths we should cling to during our pain, a key one is that our honest responses to agony and affliction are not too much for God.

> Prayers filled with the language of our tears are not too much for God.
>
> Prayers filled with fists balled and aimed at the sky are not too much for God.
>
> Prayers filled with rage that is truly grief with no place to go are not too much for God.

Job does not cover his pain with the bandages of sentiment and platitude. Instead, he confronts his pain honestly, bringing it to God and wrestling with Him in it. And his wrestling gives permission for ours, as we, too, need to grapple with the unfairness of the valley. He cries out that God has deprived him of justice and made him bitter (27:2). He goes as far as to claim that God's anger is tearing at and harassing him, and that the Lord is gnashing His teeth at him (16:9). Job gives us a vivid illustration of the inner turmoil of trying to reconcile what we are going through with what we believed to be true of God. And none of this is too much for God to handle.

This is where we see the importance of living out proper theology. Our understanding of God doesn't transform into true revelation until it's placed in the fire. We witness Job in a cyclone of emotions. Contending. Warring. Fighting with himself to not allow his wounds to make conclusions contrary to his faith. Even though Job's emotions and outbursts are all over the place, he continues to land on this sliver of belief: despite his suffering he *cannot* conclude God is *not* who He says He is.

This is also where we struggle to suffer like Job. At first, while I thought Job's response was honorable, it didn't seem relatable to me. It's difficult to face affliction the way Job does. We can read the story of Job, admire the way he responds to the pain that comes in wave after wave, and struggle to face our affliction with confidence that we are not left alone.

Though our own weariness can prompt us to interpret Job's reaction to suffering as an impossible standard, he instead illustrates what is possible when we carry our pain with God. When we remember who Christ is, we find confidence to show up to suffering as we are, to wrestle openly and honestly, and to trust that none of this is too much for God. That is the conclusion we can draw, like Job does, and we can take heart in this story because it makes space for a messy wrestling process.

The Answers We Hope Will Soothe

We follow Job through over thirty chapters of suffering. His friends are convinced that the wreckage of his life is because of his own sin. They offer explanations regarding his pain— explanations that echo what we may have heard, or even told ourselves.

I must be suffering because this is a punishment.

I must be suffering because this is a test.

I must be suffering because I didn't obey God.

I must be suffering because this is payback.

We lose strength when we obsess over the "because." Consumed with understanding why, we struggle with staying under His wings of refuge as we walk through the valley of the shadow of death. When we're more interested in the answers than His presence, we become burdened by the weight of both our suffering and our desire to know why we are suffering. It's too heavy a load to bear.

It's not wrong to want to know why, especially if the "why" keeps us in the relationship as we wrestle. Even Jesus cried, "Why, God?" from the cross. Job himself begs God to reveal the reason behind his affliction.

The answer never comes.

But God does.

God finally appears in the whirlwind. And He does not tell Job that Satan approached Him in heaven and proposed a test. He doesn't inform Job that He lowered the hedge of protection around him and allowed Satan to strip him of everything.

God tells Job about Himself.

In detail, God speaks to His power by responding to Job's questions with His own.

> Have you ever in your life commanded the morning
> or assigned the dawn its place,
> so it may seize the edges of the earth
> and shake the wicked out of it? (38:12–13)

> Where is the road to the home of light?
> Do you know where darkness lives,
> so you can lead it back to its border? (vv. 19–20)

> Who provides the raven's food
> when its young cry out to God
> and wander about for lack of food?

Do you know when mountain goats give birth?
Have you watched the deer in labor?
Can you count the months they are pregnant
so you can know the time they give birth?
   (38:41–39:2)

With each question, God confronts Job's limited under-standing of His power. And though He does not provide Job with the answer to his question, He reveals His character as true balm. We, like Job, often think the answers will bring peace. We assume this type of knowing will strengthen us. But when God appears to Job, He does not reveal the why. He reveals Himself as El Shaddai—God Almighty.

"El Shaddai" occurs in Job and Genesis more than any other biblical books. *Shaddai* speaks of "the mighty One of resource of sufficiency."[1] When we think of this name of God, we likely think it's displayed in power. But El Shaddai also speaks to God as the mighty One who can sustain us. The root word *shad* means a breast. We see this in Genesis 49:25, where God Almighty is described as the one who gives us "blessings of the breasts." Our El Shaddai is the one who can nourish and satisfy us the same way a breastfeeding mother nourishes her child. Job wants an explanation, and God gives him more. Instead of a detailed story of why he is suffering, God gives Job a detailed story of who He is as El Shaddai.

That is the only answer Job can put his trust in.

In our obsession to press on our pain until the point of explanation, we can miss God with us in our suffering al-together. There are gifts to be found in our suffering. Riches to be discovered under the rubble when we are ready to lift up the stones. Diamonds scattered on the roads we walk in pain, glistening remnants waiting for our weary hands to grab them, reminding us that it is not all in vain.

And yet God doesn't ride on explanations in order to enter our pain. We can confidently believe that nothing is wasted, not because everything is or will be answered but because in our suffering we are never left to ourselves. And this isn't a pretty slogan we slam onto our afflictions in an effort to pacify the very real experience of hurting when we know we serve a God who can make it all stop yet somehow hasn't.

Our why may go unanswered, but our groans are always heard. And, perhaps, the moment we realize He arrives even when the answers do not, we can see how His presence is an even better promise. His vow to us is not to always bring understanding but to always be with us (Isa. 43:2). His presence, His comfort, His with-ness are better by far than having any why answered, or receiving any reason we believe will make it hurt less. Hurting less is not always possible, but hurting *with* is.

Ultimately, this is the essence of suffering soft: staying awake to God's presence in our pain and letting His with-ness be real and close to us.

We Suffer to Get Well

Job shows us what it means to suffer well. And perhaps suffering in such a way is different than you've been led to believe.

It's not gritting through the agony with this idea that God takes delight in your pain. He is not a heartless King to sit and find joy in your suffering. He looks at us, in our suffering, with a longing to enter our pain with Himself, to bless our bleeding with His presence. To suffer well, to suffer soft, is to suffer *with*. Alice Walker writes of pain in a way that is both holy and human:

> Truly the suffering is great, here on earth. We blunder along, shredded by our mistakes, bludgeoned by our faults. Not having a clue where the dark path leads us. But on the whole, we stumble along bravely, don't you think?[2]

We don't preserve our softness by maintaining a gallant stride through the valley, as though the soles of our feet are not riddled with the blisters of the journey. We suffer soft by inching forward, haggardly stumbling along the path set before us. Trusting that, perhaps, our pain is not evidence of our failure. Despite what we do not want to admit, despite our insistence on the Job equation, Scripture tells us plainly: "he makes his sun rise on the evil and on the good, and sends rain on the just and on the unjust" (Matt. 5:45 ESV). Life has a way of not caring that we know God, doesn't it? It seemingly mocks our faith by pounding us deep into the earth—as if to remind us of our origins. Dust and breath. But maybe that's the point. Maybe what seems to be mocking us is meant to remind us that the world is not on our shoulders.

Walker provides a beautiful depiction of being human enough to acknowledge the pain and hopeful enough to keep going. In Mark 5:25, we learn of the woman with the issue of blood, who has suffered for many years. Like Job, she may have wondered why no physician could offer her answers or any resolution. As her condition worsens, she stumbles along bravely—week after week, month after month, year after year.

Until she sees Jesus.

His presence sparks a new hope within her. The woman tells herself, "If I touch even his garments, I will be made well" (v. 28 ESV). It's a story that propels her to push through the crowds. For her, touching just the hem of Jesus's robe becomes her wrestling with God.

The hard truth is that pain is sometimes without purpose. Like Job and like this courageous woman, we cannot always know the why. Sometimes we'll find ourselves walking through the valley of the shadow of death not because it's a test but because it simply must be walked. And it has been walked. By love Himself. Knowing this can give us the confidence of approaching Jesus—as this woman did—even as we wrestle in our pain.

We stumble along, brave enough to believe we are being sustained even when we aren't given the answers we long for. We stumble along, brave enough to refuse to reduce our suffering to an object lesson. We stumble along, singing a tune in the valley, stuffing notes into bottles that we send off to sea. Brave enough to simply be in the middle of the things we long to escape.

Job doesn't suffer well because he is exceptional. Before the hedge of protection around him is lowered, we see a glimpse of how Job walks in what God regards as "perfect integrity" (1:8).

> Whenever a round of banqueting was over, Job would send for his children and purify them, rising early in the morning to offer burnt offerings for all of them. For Job thought, "Perhaps my children have sinned, *having cursed God in their hearts.*" This was Job's regular practice. (v. 5)

Job is aware that cursing God in one's heart is sin. And despite the pain, suffering, and loss he endures, he never curses God in his heart. Even though his questions and grief cause him a great deal of inner turmoil and emotional distress, his heart remains steadfast in belief that God is still worthy of being revered as God. Our fear of God will always inform our response to situations that feel as though we are serving a cruel king. Job's questions never lead him to deny God as God; to the contrary, his wrestling leads him deeper into the mysterious character of God that grants comfort when we do not understand the reason for the pain.

The book of Job is not a guide to answer why we live devoted to God and still walk through suffering. It doesn't answer why some have to endure more than others. Or why God doesn't always provide an exit and sometimes sends us back to the path riddled with pain because the only way out is through. What Job does teach us is that when we receive the promise of suffering, the guaranteed portion of affliction, we are placed in the middle of a war within ourselves. David Guzik mentions this in his commentary on Job:

> The Book of Job is about an *epic war*. Yet no city is attacked or besieged or conquered; no battles are won or lost; no oceans are sailed, or nations founded, or adventures recorded. The whole conflict happens on an ash heap—virtually a garbage dump—outside a village. It is an epic war, but one of the inner life; a struggle to make sense of some of the deepest questions of life.[3]

To suffer well is to battle with all the things we held as truth before we bled. We wage war against the lie that our suffering is in vain. Our pain itself may or may not have a known purpose, but regardless, our suffering can always be a sacred place where we meet God. Like that of the woman who wants to get well, our suffering can lead us to a place where we encounter God in a powerful revelation of who He is.

Ultimately, as we know, God restores Job and he receives back double what he had lost. But I don't think that's the true takeaway from the story, even if it is so often told that way. To me, the greatest restoration in Job's life is the tenderness of his heart as he loses everything. By the grace of God, Job is restored to a right understanding of God.

The Job equation falls short in speaking to the complexities and nuance of affliction. This interpretation of the story can lead to language meant to comfort instead causing harm. For example, no one walking through the pain of losing a child would consider the ability to have another child an "equal replacement." How we speak of restoration in and through our suffering matters.

Maybe, like Job, you've lost much. In your suffering, your heart can crack. As you walk through the valley, you can begin to armor your heart with the layers of your own "understanding" to avoid the pain of feeling it all. But God longs to restore you to tenderness. He does not do so through flat, objective answers but through the fullness of His loving presence.

He walks with you and invites you to exchange the why for the Way. He restores you to tenderness by reminding you that though there is much you do not know about His sovereignty, what you know about His character is enough. You won't always understand why His hand moves the way it does, what He chooses to take, and what He leaves for you to hold as you are carried through, but you can trust His heart to sustain your own with compassion and mercy.

When you are tempted to regard God as a distant entity gazing on your agony with popcorn and a smirk, I hope you consider Job. Job wrestles deeply and cries "Why?" but never lets go of what he knows about God. Job, though seemingly left alone to suffer, is not. He is continually sustained, as are you. You are held and seen in your suffering.

To suffer well is to suffer with a God who longs to reveal more of Himself in the throes of our affliction. And as we hurt, we find. As we see our wounds, we are reminded of the wounds He bore not just to be with us as God but to dwell with us as the High Priest touched with the feeling of our own infirmities (Heb. 4:15). And we can hum that it truly is well with our souls to suffer with the One who suffered most. We suffer well by acknowledging that God does not use pain to make strong soldiers but to make Himself known.

9

THE MELODY IN
THE SHIPWRECK

How Tuning Your Heart to the Song of Hope Is Balm

It was a snowy day in February, a couple weeks after my thirteenth birthday, and it was time for my rite of passage. My parents asked what PG-13 movie I wanted to watch as my inauguration into cinematic adulthood. Being the hopeless romantic that I was, I chose *Titanic*. Now, when I say my parents were strict, I don't mean in a *sense* of the word—they were old-school "I'm not one of your little friends" kind of strict. And because of that, even though I was finally going to be allowed to watch a film that had some mature scenes in it, I most definitely wasn't going to see them.

My parents and I nestled ourselves onto our worn floral couch, and I was taken in by the story of how two lovers, unlikely to have ever met outside of the grandiose ship, found one another. Of course I was dismissed to the basement, where my grandparents were watching the news for the fifteenth time that day, when a scene eliciting the PG-13 rating came on. But despite that, I was glued to the screen as I watched the RMS *Titanic* slowly submerge into the ocean. I had never heard the story of the *Titanic*, so it was to me what it had been to the characters—shocking and sobering.

In one scene, as the passengers are frantically attempting to find refuge off the ship, a group of musicians calmly and boldly play their instruments as if at an opening night concert and not in an intense moment of mortal chaos. It's heartbreaking to see their art in the face of impending doom. After concluding their song, all the musicians look at each other with weary eyes and depart to join the crowd to get off the sinking ship. But the leader, Wallace Hartley (who is nameless in the film but not in the historical account), remains and continues to play. Without hesitation, the other musicians turn back, making a decision they know will end with going down with the ship. They pick up their instruments once again and play, as many survivors recalled, the 1841 hymn "Nearer My God to Thee."

Playing a melody about how God is close in the middle of a dire situation might not seem very hopeful, but I have come to think of it as one of the most authentic expressions of hope: the nearness of God.

Hope is a word we toss like confetti into the air to color the dim spaces of suffering. We are desperate that each bright piece of chopped tissue paper will bring us peace as we sit with our pain. This reduces hope into something that can never be caught, grasped, or held in our suffering. I think hope is far more than such Christianized optimism makes it out to be.

Aside from our own tribulations, there is a weariness we experience from witnessing the cruelty of this world. The headlines we read, the news we watch, even the conversations we hear and have about the tragedies among us—all have a way of chipping away at our hope. And after a while we decide our hope cannot survive in such a cruel world. We withdraw our steady confidence in what God can do and put it into only what we've come to know the world is capable of doing.

Hope is risky business, and some of us squash the flame of hope to keep from having to wrestle with the possibility of it landing us in a place not on our maps. Others carry a hope that is not strengthened by encouragement and therefore cannot sustain the heart. Proverbs 13:12 says, "Hope delayed makes the heart sick," and when that becomes a reality, in its infirmity, desperate for the remedy, the heart becomes hard.

Honest hope is what sustains our tenderness. It is honest hope—neither despair nor cheap confetti—that compelled the *Titanic* musicians to keep playing. Hope is the melody that softens us in the middle of the shipwreck. It's the song that plays when it doesn't make sense for us to sing as we are sinking.

Hope is not the fluff of our faith. It's not a term we toss in the air at any mention of hardship or any sign of suffering. Hope is not an ethereal idea that floats above our Christian lives. Hope is not, as N. T. Wright describes, a "vague and fuzzy optimism that somehow things may work out in the end."[1] But in our ignorance, in our frustration, or in our desperation to survive in a hopeless world, that is what we've reduced hope to. But hope is the melody in the midst of the shipwreck. The flicker of light in a dark room. Unlike our Western understanding of hope as being abstract, in Hebrew, hope is defined with a strong visual.

The Thread of Hope

In Hebrew, the word for hope is *tikvah*, and it's defined as an expectation and as a cord. It comes from the Hebrew root *kavah*, which means to bind together, collect; to expect— wait (for, on, and upon).[2] Hope is not a feeling, a wish, or an energy that settles on top of our desires. It is a bound-together cord that may not be seen with our eyes but can be grasped with our hands. The first mention of *tikvah* in the Bible is in the story of Rahab:

> The men said to her, "We will be free from this oath you made us swear, unless, when we enter the land, you tie this *scarlet cord* [tikvah] to the window through which you let us down. Bring your father, mother, brothers, and all your father's family into your house." (Josh. 2:17–18)

Rahab was a Canaanite woman living in Jericho. When two spies were sent to Jericho, on Joshua's command, they went to Rahab's home and she hid them. In exchange for her kindness, Rahab asked for her family to be spared when the Israelites returned to claim Jericho. Then the men instructed Rahab to hang a scarlet cord from her window as a way to mark her home as one that should be spared. After the spies had left, Rahab tied the *tikvah* (scarlet cord) to her window.

Rahab was a prostitute, yet that scarlet cord hung from her window in a radical illustration of how hope can be tied to unlikely places. It's tempting, in our deepest despair, to try to tie our hope to a sermon, or a church gathering, or an encouraging word from our favorite influencer. Or we try to tie hope to Christian jargon and the overspiritualiza- tion of suffering. But life has often proven that hope hangs where we least expect it. And perhaps we harden ourselves by attempting to tie hope where we believe it can or should thrive, instead of believing it can be tied to the miscarriage, the failed marriage, the rejection, or the hallway we sit in with various closed doors.

The scarlet cord was Rahab's hope as she waited for the spies' promise to be fulfilled. When we consider the hardening of our hearts, we often crack because the waiting begins to mock our hope. Our weariness grips our tenderness until we layer ourselves with the armor of refusing to hope again. Not because we don't want to hope but because we cannot bear the thought of risking it. This staying soft, this posture of the heart, is not the result of bearing all things but of bringing all things to the feet of the Lord.

Our hearts were made to hold hope, but when we cannot hold it, sometimes the only way to stay soft is to let hope be the cord that hangs in the window. I think of it as a flag, a wind-waved proclamation: "This we believe."

One day I sat in a quaint neighborhood café on an iron chair across from an old friend. Our coffee had grown cold, as it does when the conversation flows freely. Words covered with pain and grief swirled around the small space we occupied. After sharing a story of a recent loss, with eyes holding back tears, my friend let out a breath and a confession: "I've come to a point where I'm letting go of hope." It was a truth I'd arrived at many times. I was parked at the same rest stop she had pulled into.

That afternoon, I stared at another dear friend who sat in the ruins of shattered hope. I had sat in worship services with her, I had sat in funerals with her, I had sat in cozy living rooms with her and felt the presence of God rest on her shoulders. And I could relate to my friend that day, and her decision to let go of the bound cord. It was a decision her hurt had led her to. And though her countenance carried more grief than glory, her eyes still seemed to flicker with the small flame that "even if," there was still goodness in the rubble.

After hiding the spies, Rahab tells them, "I know that the LORD has given [Israel] this land" (Josh. 2:9). She recites all she has heard of God and the miraculous works of His hands, revealing it is because of that information she has helped them, and now she asks for a promise of protection. When we recall God's character, as Rahab did, hope is sure to follow.

There will be times when your tenderness is tied to the choice to look beyond the despair and toward the cord that will hold you even when you are not strong enough to hold it yourself. The cord of hope that runs throughout Scripture runs through your very being even now, as God is at work in your life. I think that was the flicker I saw in my friend's eyes that day; even when she felt she could not hold on any longer, the hope of God was holding her.

Rahab put forth the scarlet cord of hope after considering what she knew to be true of God, and the world remembers her for her faith. When life is at its hardest, we can follow her by being brave enough to look for threads of hope hanging in unlikely places.

Hope Personified

I remember flinching whenever someone would try to comfort me with the mention of hope. Did they not know what I had been through? Didn't they see my pain? The comfort hope promised to bring felt cruel. As people tried to cover me with their optimism, it brushed against my skin like scratchy sandpaper. Hope presented to me like confetti made me harden my heart, not because to hope was wrong but because I was convinced to hope was to deny the very real wrong I had experienced.

Hope was just an idea.
Hope was a concept I knew much of cognitively but
   didn't know experientially.
Hope was confetti to sprinkle over my head as a religious ritual.
Hoping was wishing for better without making mention
   of the ache.

As you work your way through this chapter, you may come to realize that your heart is hardened to hope. Not because you believe hopelessness is the better way. You long to be reacquainted with the warmth that comes with believing for better, but life has let you down too many times.

But what if you haven't lost hope but rather lost the true meaning of what hope is? What if what has slipped through your fingers is a spiritual version of optimism and not the substance of hope itself—thick with the blood of Christ and the glory of His resurrection?

In her poem "'Hope' is the thing with feathers," Emily Dickinson compares hope to a small bird that sings in the midst of a powerful storm. Her metaphor illustrates hope as something that speaks to us in an unconventional way. Hope is always present and always singing; it can always be heard even when the fierce storms of life make it hard to see.

As beautiful as Dickinson's metaphor is, hope is not just a bird that sings. Hope is a person who lives. Hope is alive because Jesus is alive. And your "living hope" (1 Pet. 1:3) smooths the parts of your heart cracked by disappointment and despair. Your living hope has His eyes on your ache for what didn't come—with the foresight to know what is on the way. In Dickinson's poem, the word *hope* is nestled between quotation marks, begging the question that, perhaps, she is offering the reader the opportunity to consider how hope is defined. And when we define hope as the living and breathing Spirit of God, the poem reads even more beautifully.

> [*The Spirit of God*] is the thing with feathers—
> that perches in the soul—
> And sings the tune without the words—
> And never stops—at all—[3]

Hope is not a fickle thing, despite what you may have been told. Somewhere along the way, disappointment may have convinced you that it's safer to dodge the very thing you need. It pushes you to believe that hope lies fragile in your battered hand when the truth is *you* are a fragile being in the Father's hand.

If hope is the song that never stops playing, when the melody is hushed it's because we have stopped listening. But the good news for those who've grown deaf is that though a hard heart may hinder our ability to sense and surrender to hope, it can never silence hope's song. There is no despair great enough to silence the voice of Hope Himself. No disappointment so daunting it can rid the earth of the melody that never stops playing.

Our lives can't afford a hope that's been reduced to an idea without breath, a concept without character, or a principle that lacks personhood. Hope personified can do what even the brightest confetti cannot: soften a heart marred by disappointment and cracked from despair.

Before Hope took on human flesh, God was silent for four hundred years of history. Paul describes the desperate state of humanity: "without hope and without God in the world" (Eph. 2:12), a body with hung head and worn knees.

Some died waiting. Some lived with the sting of having hoped for what felt like too long. But Hope was born in a manger, with stars singing in the thick of the darkness. Hope was cradled in the hands of a teenage virgin girl. Hope held the cries of an infant and the playfulness of a child. As a mother who knows the anguish of labor, I know Hope was brought into the earth through tears and groans. We can relate to Hope's arrival in the same fashion: birthed from pain, sown with tears, and released as a groan. Hope was a man who walked among the flesh He created. Hope was a man who carried His cross to Calvary and died to restore a people back to Himself. Hope was and is and is to come.

Hope is Jesus, and as such, Hope is always here for us.

Still, those who walked with Jesus in first-century Israel had their own moment of believing all hope was lost.

Jesus walked among humankind as a living hope to those who waited over thirteen generations for His arrival. He came as He promised—but not like they expected. And then the King who was supposed to redeem Israel by rescuing God's people from the grip of their oppressors died. Now, several days later, Hope is believed to be sitting in a tomb—wrapped in burial clothes and left to decay. Cleopas and his friend, both disciples of Jesus, are carrying their heavy feet back to their village, Emmaus, from Jerusalem, a journey of about seven miles. The walk is long enough to discuss "everything that had taken place" (Luke 24:14). Long enough to discuss the devastation of watching their living hope hung on a tree. They walk along a path stripped of hope, unaware that the tomb that held it is now empty. There's much to be said about Hope personified in Luke's retelling of Christ meeting these disciples on the road to Emmaus. The two disciples have hearts fragmented by despair, but Hope finds them on the dusty roads of disappointment.

The two disciples have just witnessed a traumatizing death. They've seen what they saw, just like you have. The divorce papers sitting on the kitchen table. The fifth negative pregnancy test positioned on the counter. The rejection email glowing through the computer screen in the middle of the night. The door that still hasn't flung open to reveal the child you prayed would return. The death of all you've hoped for. They saw. And the thing is, they've also heard rumors that the tomb is in fact empty. A hope heard before it's held. The song of hope singing before the presence of Hope arrives.

> As they talked and discussed these things with each other, Jesus himself came up and walked along with them; but they were kept from recognizing him. (vv. 15–16 NIV)

Jesus appears and quietly bears witness to the grief of these two men as they continue to walk. Hope made flesh doesn't just hover over us, demanding we respond as we should. We don't have to be quick to scurry to hope when we have been stripped of our ability to look to the future with the promise in mind. No—the promise has a way of finding *us* on the dusty road of our broken lives. And Hope speaks when our own words try to tangle us up in our sorrow.

> Then he asked them, "What is this dispute that you're having with each other as you are walking?" And they stopped walking and looked discouraged.
>
> The one named Cleopas answered him, "Are you the only visitor in Jerusalem who doesn't know the things that happened there in these days?"
>
> "What things?" he asked them. (vv. 17–19)

Jesus asks them what happened not because He doesn't know, obviously, but because He's creating space for their honesty. It's as though every confession of truth regarding their pain massages the parts of their hearts that are hardened with hopelessness.

This is what Hope personified always does: it meets us right where we are. God, in His love, after bearing witness to the tears we've cried—in the closet, in the bathroom as our children slept, into the sink as we washed the dishes—then waits for us to tell *Him* the story of our hurt. He asks them "What things?" in the same way He would ask "What let you down?" and "What hurt the most?" And though telling the truth doesn't always cause the brilliance of hope to spring forth, it does clear the dust so we can see what can become.

The disciples respond to Jesus and tell Him the facts of what happened interlaced with their own confession of what it means to them. A retelling of what died on the cross that night and what also died in them.

> So they said to him, "The things concerning Jesus of Nazareth, who was a prophet powerful in action and speech before God and all the people, and how our chief priests and leaders handed him over to be sentenced to death, and they crucified him. But we were hoping that he was the one who was about to redeem Israel. Besides all this, it's the third day since these things happened." (vv. 19–21)

We were hoping. These three words are some of the saddest and most heartbreaking words in all of Scripture. I've felt the weight of these words. They've climbed up my throat as my eyes burned with the tears I tried to hold back before they fell painfully. Cleopas echoes the same sentiment as Martha when Jesus arrives at the tomb of her brother: "Lord, if you had been here" (John 11:21 ESV).

Our hearts don't crack purely from hope deferred. Yes, the waiting can bring forth its own wailing. But there's a profound pain that pours out of us when we find ourselves under the weight of disappointment because God didn't come when we thought He would.

The disciples had hoped Jesus would redeem Israel the way *they* expected Him to do it. They tell Jesus about Himself, referring to Him as a powerful prophet. Their hope was waist deep in who they desired Jesus of Nazareth to be: a king sent to overpower their oppressor. *They had hoped* in a Jesus they created in the image of their own desire. *They had hoped* in a Jesus they had to watch be beaten and nailed to a cross.

How was this redemption? How was this the answer they had waited for generations to appear? How could it be that after over four hundred years of clinging to hope, hope fulfilled became hope crucified?

Jesus has a way of coming when what we've defined as hope is gone. In John 11, when Jesus learns His friend Lazarus is ill, He waits before going to visit. He waits until Lazarus has been dead for four days, to be exact. Jewish superstition at the time said that a soul stayed close to the grave for three days. This superstition created a sense of hope. But Jesus waits.

Four days have passed. Any fragment of hope has dissipated. But then Jesus. When it seems all hope is lost, Hope incarnate appears at the tomb. When it seems all hope is lost, Hope incarnate appears on the road to Emmaus. When it seems all hope is lost, Hope incarnate appears for us. His presence is the balm when we whisper "We had hoped," and "If you had been here." And when we are tempted to conclude that there is no hope, we cast our eyes on Him who is Hope. And He finds us. Hope finds us on the dusty roads and near the graves we've watched with mourning.

Our living hope finds us, declaring He is not afraid of dead things.

Hope is the miracle of being found on the dusty road between where we went with expectation and where we return with disappointment. The miracle of Emmanuel walking with us as we lament. It springs up as we whisper to a God who can hold our disappointment and resurrect our hope.

Softened to Hear

Romans 5 says, "And hope does not put us to shame, because God's love has been poured out into our hearts through the Holy Spirit, who has been given to us" (v. 5 NIV). Why would

Paul allude to a sense of shame coming to those who are courageous enough to hope?

Because misplaced hope can lead to disappointment. Hope in a specific outcome can cripple us with shame. But there is a hope that never disappoints. The hope that is God with us. Hoping in Hope Himself will never lead to disappointment. And to sink our anchor down into the ocean of His character is an act of bravery that will never be in vain. Our deepest assurance can be found in who He is, and this will never let us down.

Here's the truth that I pray covers you: the softening is in letting Hope find you on the dusty road between what you desired and your disappointment. It's in slowing down, in the middle of the shipwreck, to find the melody that was there all along. The softening is not in throwing Christian confetti over your devastation or rushing to hope when you have not reckoned with your despair.

Hope will find you as God seeks you out in active pursuit. Even when you wish God had come sooner and when you wish God had come differently, you may be softened by the miracle of being found. Hope makes us tender by meeting us where we are and tuning our hearts to the song that never stopped playing.

10

THE GATHERING OF SOFT HEARTS

How God Softens Us Back toward Belonging

I drove a fifteen-passenger van to Vermont for a spring break mission trip during my freshman year of college. Unlike students who filled the beaches of Cancun, there were those of us from Christian schools who embarked on the "Lord's work" during this blessed break. For me, this trip was more than a way to signal to my own virtue and check off my "goodwill" box for the year. I had been selected, after interviewing, to lead a group of upperclassmen and a few other freshmen for this trip. And the icing on the cake of being in charge (which was my favorite thing to be) was that my crush was part of the group. The missionary kid from Cambodia who I wanted desperately to choose me.

The trip was what one would expect a mission trip to be. We worked during the day serving the ministry and doing the work we had sacrificed our break for. And for me, evenings were filled with time with the boy I was sure would leave this mission trip convinced that choosing me was the best and obvious choice. He just needed a little nudge. One night, I found myself in the small cabin with him and his friend. They were discussing something I wasn't interested in, ignoring my existence, and I kept myself warm with the fact that I was lucky to be in his presence.

Suddenly, the boy with whom I had, at this point, mentally built a whole life with, turned to me and said something I would find myself repeating to myself whenever rejection showed up in my life.

"Charaia, you're like a dog toy."

The comment caught me off guard. It was mean enough to knock the wind out of me but with a hint of absurdity that gave me enough doubt to not be fully offended.

"Well, what do you mean?" I smiled faintly, rolling the fibers of the carpet between my fingers.

"You're just always here. Always around. A dog toy that I can just pick up whenever I want."

The blow of rejection took my breath away. I thought I was on the cusp of being chosen, and the possibility had drowned out the doubt that I would never be worthy of being wanted. I thought the times earlier in the week when he'd reached for my hand under the blanket as we watched a movie meant something. I thought the walks in the rain we took before this trip, when he whispered how he felt, meant something. But now it was clear that he wasn't choosing me because I was worth being chosen. He was simply picking up what was in his path. Taking advantage of what was available.

I was so desperate to be wanted that, though I left the cabin that night after expressing my disgust with his comment, I still wanted him. I still wanted the plague of loneliness I felt I was suffering from to end by hearing him declare I was the one. But he closed the door to that hope. The boy did write me an apology the next day, confessing that everything that had transpired between us was a big mistake, and that he thought friendship was the better option. But when we returned to school, his avoidance of me sent the clear signal that even that door was closed.

I could list story after story of rejection. And each door in my life that slammed reminded me that belonging was a pointless desire and being wanted was an impossible reality. The sound of a door slamming became the soundtrack of my life. I kept my heart hardened to the community I most desired because I believed it was the thing I least deserved—and it was easier that way. Behind the image of self-reliance and independence I portrayed was a younger me afraid to believe she was worth being kept, not only by God but by others. Hardening my heart to the idea of community was safer.

We've all been hurt by the very communities we thought we'd be safe in. We've all written new stories from rejection that has made it hard to believe community is worth it. And it seems easier to check out of community altogether to avoid the risk instead of persisting until we find where we can belong.

But the invitation to bravely step into an open door of community when previous doors have slammed in our faces is always extended toward us. The question is, How can we stay soft to each other, stay open to relationship, after relationships have been the source of great pain? Our hurt has a way of hurling us to the outskirts of community. Yet God has a way of making us tender in the solitude by using it to teach us our identity as His beloved. And when we step back into the context of healthy fellowship, the act of being gathered by the softness of others massages out the sharp edges left on our hearts after breaking.

Reckoning with Rejection in the Hallway

Life has proven that rejection is often a brutal bully that towers over me as the manifestation of every lie I've tried to outrun. Its intimidating presence mocks my audacity to try to belong again.

We try to explain away rejection because we believe we can soothe the sting of slamming doors by flipping rejection into a divine reroute. But underneath this tendency is a truer story: rejection simply hurts too much to see past it.

Rejection does not always lead us immediately to an open door, or into the arms of someone ready to receive us. Rejection isn't always a gentle guide that points to a better way. However, if we are to believe that rejection can provide redirection, we must consider that sometimes we'll be redirected back to the hallway. To reckon with the sermon of the slamming of doors. To decide, then, in the middle of being turned away, which voices are worth listening to.

We'll never be able to reject rejection. It's inevitable. But as doors shut, we can reject the stories they attempt to write. We can admit the threat to our tenderness and preach to ourselves a new sermon contrary to the one we want to sit under after the pain comes.

I know what it's like to be hurt into an ending. To experience door after door shutting in my face and resolve that trying to belong is to risk the taste of rejection my palate has become accustomed to. And it is indeed a scary thing to believe that the desire to belong is not something we can graduate from as we grow in our sense of security. But it's from a secure and soft heart that we can lean into the terrifying, beautiful, risky business of letting ourselves be seen by broken people.

In the aftermath of rejection, we are tempted to turn the agony into a vow:

I'll shut the door before someone can shut it in my face.
I'd rather be alone than risk being rejected.
I don't need anyone, and I'll never rely on anyone again.

We make promises from our hurt that keep us from the healing power of belonging. We detach from relationships because we anticipate the worst. We believe being alone is better because we're afraid the people who shut doors on us in the past speak for every person behind any other door in our future. And we then make the inevitable conclusion that we do not need anyone. Not because we've successfully smothered our desire to belong but because we believe we're not needed.

When we refuse to reckon in the hallway, we think we can protect ourselves by rejecting ourselves before others get the chance to. We think we can avoid the sting of a shutting door by being the one to grab the handle and close it ourselves. We don't just anticipate abandonment; we attach our identity to the absence of belonging, telling ourselves that being on the outside is part of who we are.

Now, the danger with simply believing "rejection is redirection" is that it lacks the nuance needed to speak to the effects of rejection and to do the very real work that can be done in the hallway. Rejection is not just something to "bounce back" from; it marks us. It can propel us toward the conclusion that someone's inability to love us well is indicative of our worth: *If they did not accept us, surely God does not accept us, either.*

If we refuse to pause after the door slams, we miss the chance for God to heal the hurt that so often leads us to make such self-sabotaging vows. When we skip the reckoning in the hallway, we miss the miracle that happens when God enters our solitude—when we expel the false narrative of rejection and return to the sacred Voice who calls us beloved.

The Solitude Where Our Softening Starts

It had been almost six months since my kids and I relocated from Georgia to Colorado. It was the second time I'd sought refuge in my home state within the last two years, but this time we were returning to stay. I didn't picture the transition being as lonely as it was. After a few months of staying with different family members, I finally settled into my first home as a single mother. The days were heavy, and every one had a dusting of despair on top of it.

Nights were torture. I wasn't familiar with this type of silence. It was thick and taunting. I'd thought things would be different. I'd imagined I would get off the plane and be received by arms proud that I'd done the hard thing. I knew others had whispered about my situation, knowing what I needed to do before I was ready to see it. I'd pictured my phone filled with texts from old friends who'd attended my wedding asking when they could see me, because I wanted to be seen. I wanted someone to bear witness to my suffering and tell me I didn't deserve what was happening to me. But silence was my only visitor most of the time. She met me night after night, as if to tell me I had to bear her presence in order to move on. And in a sense, I did. I found myself face-to-face with what I'd spent two years trying to avoid: being alone with myself.

Solitude was where my heart was softened. It was where I had to wage war against the side of myself that wanted to collect the silence, the absence of others, the ultimate rejection by the love of my life, and sew them together into a garment of unworthiness. It was in this solitude of the hallway, as I replayed all the times doors had slammed on me, that Christ met me.

It's in solitude that we are caught by the hands of God. That the chanting of the shutting doors is interrupted by the melody of being called His beloved.

The solitude makes space for us to get reacquainted with our deepest identity of daughter, son, beloved child. It is a powerful thing to be called by your true name in the voice of love.

For both of my children, I remember the day they became aware of their own name. The moment I whispered it over them as I cradled their hours-old bodies, I knew who they were. But they did not. Then came the days when I would grab their little toes as they lay on the bed, looking into their eyes and whispering "Stella!" "Ezra!" Their coos and smiles were still filled with unknowing. But then came a day when they knew their own name. I would call to them and they would respond. But more than that, they knew what it meant when I called them.

We also see a powerful story of responding to our true names in the Gospel of John. In John 20, Mary Magdalene is standing outside of Jesus's tomb, weeping the kind of tears that make you weak:

> As she was crying, she stooped to look into the tomb. She saw two angels in white sitting where Jesus's body had been lying, one at the head and the other at the feet. They said to her, "Woman, why are you crying?"
>
> "Because they've taken away my Lord," she told them, "and I don't know where they've put him."
>
> Having said this, she turned around and saw Jesus standing there, but she did not know it was Jesus. "Woman," Jesus said to her, "why are you crying? Who is it that you're seeking?"
>
> Supposing he was the gardener, she replied, "Sir, if you've carried him away, tell me where you've put him, and I will take him away."
>
> Jesus said to her, "Mary."
>
> Turning around, she said to him in Aramaic, "Rabboni!"—which means "Teacher." (vv. 11–16)

Jesus speaks to Mary, but she does not recognize him. Some say Mary does not recognize Jesus because she's so overcome with emotion. Her emotions cloud her reason, as she believes she could somehow carry the dead body of the Messiah. Others say it's because Jesus's resurrected body is different from before. Though He bears the markings of His crucifixion, the glory of His resurrection altered Him to the point of being unrecognizable. Either way, Mary does not know she's speaking to her Lord.

Then He says her name.

One word holds a whole sermon. One word holds a deep well of revelation. God could have chosen any way to reveal Himself to Mary. He could have ascended to the heavens at that moment. He could have pointed to His scars. He could have simply said, "I AM LORD." But as R. C. Trench observes, "Jesus didn't reveal Himself to Mary by telling her who *He* was, but by telling her who *she* was to Him."[1]

Mary knows Jesus. She knows what her name sounds like from His mouth, like my kids know the sound of their names from mine. She is a sheep who knows the voice of her Shepherd. There are times we need to remind ourselves of who God is. But the hallway—after we are thrown aside, cast out, or evicted from the place of belonging—is the space in which God tells us about *who we are* to Him.

When Jesus calls us by name, He speaks to our whole being. In the hallway, we must contend against the hardening of naming ourselves according to how we were mishandled by others.

My couch became soaked with the tears I wept over the many doors that had closed in my life. And while I wanted company and the comfort of witness and community, the silence was where my heart was made tender, because that is where God met me. It was in the secret place my ears tuned themselves to the Voice that called me His. Henri Nouwen explains the transformative nature of knowing we are beloved:

> Every time you feel hurt, offended, or rejected, you have to dare to say to yourself: "These feelings, strong as they may

be, are not telling me the truth about myself. The truth, even though I cannot feel it right now, is that I am the chosen child of God, precious in God's eyes, called the Beloved from all eternity, and held safe in an everlasting embrace."[2]

That's the softening of solitude. Only God can call us by the name that can never be taken by the rejection of others—beloved. Our knee-jerk reaction after a door slams is to refuse to let ourselves be gathered as His beloved, to dig our heels into the vow of never trusting anyone again.

But divine solitude is not meant to be the place where we stomp out our desire to belong. It's not where we engage in a false sense of bravery by denying our need for fellowship or demonizing our longing to be fully seen and loved.

Perhaps the greatest way you can take care of yourself in hard times is to put on your "belovedness." Even when others have shut you out, you can care for yourself with the revelation that the sacrifice Christ made brought you into the fold. Even when others reject you, you can heal by being held by "the everlasting arms" (Deut. 33:27). God never stops choosing you even when others do. Perhaps to care for yourself is to rest in communion with the Father. Perhaps it's this type of sacred self-care that makes you tender enough to walk into rooms with the belief you are worthy of belonging.

Solitude makes space for us to get well acquainted with a Savior who catches our tears. It teaches us the softening that happens when we allow ourselves to be gathered by His hands after we've been let go of by others. God enters the secret places of our solitude with the intention to heal the beliefs our wounds can construct that keep us from seeking fellowship.

Those Who Are Gathered Gather

Summers in Georgia are brutal. After my first one, I developed some summer survival rules.

Rule #1: Keep the blinds closed.
Rule #2: Refrain from using the oven—GRILL!
Rule #3: Run the A/C at all times.

So I knew something was awry when I woke up in a pool of sweat one morning in August, the hottest month of the year. I walked out of my room, and the silence told me everything I needed to know. I couldn't hear the outside condenser unit, and when I looked the fans weren't spinning—our A/C was out.

I called my landlord, but he informed me that a technician wouldn't be able to come until the next day. He advised me to purchase a portable unit, but I knew that was impossible, as we only had enough for groceries until the next paycheck.

I had recently joined a virtual Bible study with some women I met on Instagram. Our weekly meetings were becoming something I looked forward to, especially since I hadn't made any friends since we moved. There was a group chat in which many of the women would ask for prayer from the group. I typically only popped in to say I was praying; I struggled with making my own requests. That day I was at the end of myself, and I just wanted to feel the comfort of laying something down.

I grabbed my phone and started a message with "I know this is stupid but . . ." before asking for prayer about our A/C. My phone dinged as they all responded.

Praying

Got you girl

Praying for ya

When the tech did arrive, it was only to inform me that a part had to be ordered in order to fix the unit. It may have been because I was so hot or the fact that I was solo parenting, but this lack of A/C felt like the end of the world. I picked up my phone again and typed a long message into the group chat about how overwhelmed I was, then hit send.

It was dead silent for twenty minutes. I began to regret my decision to open myself up.

Then my phone rang.

"Hello?" I tried to put some pep in my voice to mask my exhaustion.

"Hey! So, the girls and I were talking and we want to send you the money to get a window A/C unit."

Immediately I felt ashamed. *They must think I'm poor or a charity case*, I thought. *They probably think I sent that text to get them to help me*. I was so conditioned by past rejection that their generosity triggered me. I quickly thought of an excuse, because they were clearly mistaken in thinking I was worth their kindness.

"Oh, girl, I'm good. I'm not allowed to put a unit in my window. But thanks anyway! The kids and I will be good."

I was used to this kind of deflection working. But this time it didn't.

"Hmm," she began. "Ok, well, why don't we put you all in a hotel for a night so you can get some rest?"

A tear fell from my eye. Why were they being so kind to

me? Why weren't they confirming the story I had told my-self that I was a burden? That I was too much? That I wasn't worth the effort? I was taken aback by this display of love, this fruit of community. And I was so tired of pretending I could do this alone. I didn't believe I was worthy of this gift, but I wanted to dive into the warmth of this love.

"I don't know what to say, but that would be wonderful," I whispered.

There are parts of our hearts that can only be made tender in the context of community. For all the ways we've been hurt, for all the vows of self-sufficiency we've made, the truth is we need each other.

While solitude makes space for us to hear the voice of love and remember our deepest identity as God's beloved, you and I are not made to remain alone. And once we've anchored ourselves in who we truly are, we can find new courage to venture back out into the risk of relationships.

No matter how much good self-care you practice on your own, you cannot love yourself out of your need to be loved. It is a risk to knock on doors of relationships. It is a risk to answer the invitation that calls out to you as you sit in the hallway. But the risk of rejection is worth the reward of belonging.

I had spent a great deal of time trying to mend myself, but I ached to be seen, to be gathered in my broken state. And God knew this. He sent people to cover and gather me. He used this outpouring of love that found its way to me and gathered me up to soften me in a way He could not outside of relationship. The truth is, God can soften us by surrounding us with friends who show up for us in our low-est moments. It is a humbling yet beautiful thing to realize that we need each other, after all. And choosing to believe we are worthy of those who care for us with the care of God is a courageous thing.

In Mark 2:1–7, we find the story of such caring friends. A paralyzed man is brought to a home where Jesus is teaching. His friends have faith that if they can get their friend in front of Jesus, he will walk again. The home is packed with people, and the only way in is through the roof. They dig through it until there is a hole big enough to lower their friend through. No matter what rejection has convinced you of, and despite the contentment you may have found in being alone, you both need and are worthy of friends who will lower the mat for you. You are worthy of being surrounded by people who will love you enough to carry you to the feet of Christ. Who have faith when yours is frail.

We are meant to be carried on the mat and to be carriers for others. The healing we hope for is on the other side of being loved out loud. And to deny ourselves of this, to demonize this longing, is to harden part of our hearts because we are afraid we don't deserve it.

The Spirit offers us soft hearts by presenting us with twin flowers: love for God and love for others. Both provide an aroma that makes us tender when we don't believe we are worthy. Soft hearts are alive with love for others and love for God. And while the tendency to shut out others out of self-protection is understandable, we were made for more.

That is the miracle of being gathered and doing the gathering. The hardness of our hearts can be melted and made soft again by the hospitality of our neighbors, if we can find our courage to let them into our lives. If we hold fast to our vows of self-sufficiency and so strand ourselves in the hallway, we will miss the gift. Yet if we find the courage to stay soft, we can receive their gift of a safe place to land.

Those who are soft handle those who ache with care. And in this way, the gift keeps giving, as we open the doors of our lives to each other with great grace and care. God is the first to meet us in the hallway of rejection, but His heart for us is to bring us back into community with those who will care for us as He does.

The gathering of saints is meant to be a blessing, not a burden. Our community can be something to heal *within* and not something to heal *from*. The story changes, the vows are renounced, and we live as His beloved, welcoming the love of our neighbors without thinking we're unworthy and displaying the glory of softness by gathering others ourselves.

11

THE GOOD FIGHT

The Courageous Battle to Stay Soft

This book was my fight.

A good fight.

I've had author friends tell me that every book they've written has made its way through them. After living out this dream of mine, I can say there is nothing truer. This message has made its way through me; some portions are still sitting in the basement of my soul, waiting for when I'm ready to invite them up to sit at my dinner table.

I remember when staying soft became my personal anthem. It was a phrase that felt like a security blanket covering my inner child—the girl who felt as though softness would only lead to her demise. I've thought of her often in this process, wishing I could visit her and let her know that her softness led to many things, many hard and holy and beautiful things—but never to her demise. This message felt fitting for our times but also felt like it was my book to write. I suppose that's what all authors want and what we all believe: that we are the ones to tell the tales we needed to read ourselves.

Even now, as I've come to the end of this book, I'm not as tender as I hope to become. Or, at least, I recognize that becoming soft is the journey of a lifetime, not something we ever "arrive" at but something God is continually working within us. More than anything, the story I was living through as I wrote these pages was hell-bent on making a hard heart out of me.

It was maybe a week after I signed the book deal. The dream, the hard work, and the dedication had all come to fruition. I was still with my husband and waited on his celebration, but it never came. He hugged me and smiled, whispered, "I knew you could," and that was that. I went to Publix and purchased myself some flowers. While I walked to my car, the urge to cry came over me. By the time I climbed into the driver's seat, my tears were mixing with the sweat from the Georgia heat. *This was supposed to be different.*

A few weeks later, what I had feared appeared at five in the morning while my children and husband slept. What I discovered confirmed that the smoke I had been smelling, the sense I had been feeling, was real. Later in the morning, when I confronted my husband, he looked at me with eyes that had lost all familiarity and said the phrase I knew was coming:

"I want a divorce, Charaia. There's nothing left."

The next weeks were a blur, but soon enough my kids and I were back in Colorado, staying in the basement of whatever family member would take us in. I felt like my life was mocking the words I was set to write. The message I pitched to publishers months prior felt disingenuous. I was writing a book about staying soft with a heart that had transformed so radically it didn't need to stay soft, it needed to *become* soft all over again.

If it takes a miracle to cultivate a tender heart in a hard world, it takes a second miracle to *stay* tender in a world that does not bend for us. A soft heart is sustained and formed only through a fight. We must fight to stay soft—and this is perhaps the fight of our lives. I know it has been the fight of mine.

When he was little, my son would run to me when he was hurt. Any type of pain flung him right into my arms. Scraped knee, scratched elbow, bump on the head—he believed I was the one to run to when life gave him a beating. But once he turned five, something changed. Somewhere along the way, his reaction when he was hurt became to withdraw. To not want to be held, to not want to run into my arms. It hurt me deeply. I realized that his inner dialogue had established new rules of engagement: *When I hurt, I don't want to be held.*

The day I recognized this shift was a day of deep revelation of how I was keeping myself from encountering the goodness left even in the mess of my suffering and pain.

I think back to the times when being held by God was the last thing I wanted.

There is a weariness that comes from fighting to stay tender in a world bent on making us hard. We grow weary of choosing to forgive when what we want is vengeance. We grow weary of fighting to see the good when it seems our skepticism has veiled our eyes. We grow weary of hoping when all hope seems lost. And we can, in our weariness, consider staying soft to be just another thing we say but don't fight to do.

Yes, it takes courage to stay soft.

Yes, we must resist the urge to rip our hearts out of the Savior's palm and shield them by our own means. But the true fight we will find ourselves engaging in time and time again is the fight to revive the miracle of being made and being kept soft. If we're not careful, we can begin to believe that our softness is a credit to ourselves and not the miracle of God in our lives. If we're not careful, we will echo the philosophy of the world: that the worst things that have happened to us made us strong through making us soft. That we, in our own resolve, carry a tenderness that makes us exceptional. But to claim such things is to reject the miracle that God is touching our hearts after the worst things have happened.

The truth about our tender hearts is they are made when we come to the end of ourselves. A tender heart is not what we create in and of ourselves. When our self-righteousness, our cynicism, our withholding of forgiveness, and our self-reliance cannot protect or produce a tender heart, we must admit our need for a miracle—and that can only come from outside ourselves.

The hammer of life that comes down on us beats us for the sake of beating us. Life will pound us into a pulp without rhyme or reason, leaving us reeling and asking why. Life doesn't care about the outcome of each blow. But God, in His goodness and mercy, offers us a remedy for the senselessness. The pain will come, the hurt will happen, but by the grace of God, we can be made tender by the very things that could make us tough. God will always meet us in our pain, and what we might see as senseless, He can transform into invitations to be made soft.

It's never an accident to arrive at the end of a day, at the end of a season, at the end of a life with a heart that is soft toward God and humanity. It's not happenstance but a willingness to allow God to enter the rooms we've locked and touch the sin we've justified.

Honey and Wildfire

I cannot with a clear conscience conclude this book without sharpening my message. We've talked a lot about the ways God longs to make us soft and about the charge to stay soft, and now I want to clarify what staying soft is not.

Staying soft is *not* staying for the sake of proving God is at work in us. God can work in the leaving of a toxic relationship, community, or environment, and we can be soft in our choosing to walk away.

Staying soft is *not* putting on the posture of a doormat. Being made tender is not the same as being made flat, trampled beneath the weight of harm. There is a strength in our soft hearts that enables us to say *this far and no farther*. We find refuge in His wisdom, which sometimes calls us to protect ourselves with lines drawn in the sand and with boundaries.

Staying soft is *not* staying silent. It's having the courage to speak the truth with the tenderness to speak it with grace. It's restraint and wisdom. It's maturity to concern ourselves with how we speak, not just with what we have to say. Our softness carries strength to echo the voices of heaven as we speak of justice and contend for peace.

Staying soft is *not* playing nice. It does not manifest in pleasing people. Staying soft is not being a victim to the beatings of life. It's not living with bent back and lowered head, waiting for the next gut punch.

Instead, staying soft is resilience that acts like water: fierce enough to cut through rock and gentle enough to keep us afloat. A soft heart is still a force. When we are inclined to think that a soft heart in a cruel world is a weakness, may we be reminded of the principle of the kingdom of God:

> Instead, God has chosen what is foolish in the world to shame the wise, *and God has chosen what is weak in the world to shame the strong*. God has chosen what is insignificant and despised in the world—what is viewed as nothing—to bring to nothing what is viewed as something, so that no one may boast in his presence. . . . Let the one who boasts, boast in the Lord. (1 Cor. 1:27–29, 31)

Many consider the preservation of a soft heart foolish. They deem those who walk with tender hearts toward life and others as cowards when they are the courageous ones. The world is bent on marveling at the force that is a wildfire, but they miss the force that is honey in a world that aches for the sweet nectar of God. God has chosen the honey of a soft heart to shame the "strength" of a hardened heart.

The Good Fight of Guarding the Fountain

In Proverbs 4:23, Solomon writes instruction to "keep your heart with all vigilance, for from it flow the springs of life" (ESV). A heart "kept" is fought for, and one of the most worthwhile fights of our lives. A new "heart of flesh" (Ezek. 36:26) is worthy of being guarded. And we keep our hearts by being kept in the hands of God. Diligently. It's not easy to avoid a hard heart, but it is our duty to fight to remain kept, to stay held. When the wellspring of our lives is a soft heart, we possess the power to live from our tenderness and not from our circumstances. When pain and hurt hit us, we can guard the fountain that flows from the heart by telling it to stay in the direction of softness.

In the Song of Songs, the speaker interrupts the romantic conversation with his lover to offer a warning:

> Catch the foxes for us—
> the little foxes that ruin the vineyards—
> for our vineyards are in bloom. (Song 2:15)

Solomon's ancient audience would have understood that these foxes were symbolic as animals that would destroy the vineyard. You've likely done the work to be made soft and your "vineyards are in bloom." But you must fight to do the work of rounding up the foxes that can spoil the vineyard of your tender heart. And like the verse suggests, these foxes are little. They represent things we overlook and don't deem real threats. Things that are small in nature but still possess the ability to spoil the vines. And the Spirit of God equips us with the discernment to see the little critters for what they really are.

Your "little foxes" might be too much time on social media, and guarding yourself might mean actively opting out of being discipled by uncharitable hot takes. You might guard your fountain by choosing to leave the virtual "pews" of those who can only pastor our outrage.

Or maybe your little foxes come when you use Jesus as an accessory and make Him the mascot of your politics, opinions, and agendas, making yourself hard to the lordship of God.

Then there are the little foxes of the company you keep who make it hard to also keep a soft heart. Or the little foxes of envy that look at the favor of others and conclude that God is holding out on you. Or the little foxes of unbelief that seek to nibble on the harvest of hope in the wake of disappointment.

We guard the fountain of the heart by keeping watch for such "little" things and being quick to round them up and diligent to keep them from entering. We cannot remain tender through a passive defense. Our innermost fountain is precious, and our defense must be active and continual.

I truly believe that the life we long for—the joy, the abundance, the peace—is found in courageously guarding a soft heart. And when we fall off course, when the fountains of our soft hearts become polluted, we do the work of inviting the Spirit to purify us and make us tender once again.

Join me in committing to a life of becoming and staying soft as we live between the garden and glory. We stay soft until we embrace an eternity when our hearts will never turn hard again, when we enter into that paradise where softness doesn't have to be fought for because pain and suffering can no longer make us hard. And our own sin can no longer choke out what God has made tender. We fight until we enter glory. We fight to display the glory of a tender heart in a tough world.

We partake of the miracle of staying soft until we meet the One who kept us soft all along.

ACKNOWLEDGMENTS

To Ezra and Stella: I wrote this book in your midst. I wrote it while you played outside, in between meals, during naps, and on the bathroom floor while you splashed in the tub. You are the reason I fought and continue to fight to keep my heart tender. I love you with all my heart, and I pray you read this book and can say that it lines up with the life I've lived in our home. You two are my everything. Thank you for being my reason to keep going.

To Shaina and Anisha: you are my built-in best friends. Thank you for carrying me through the darkest seasons of my life. You believed in me when I didn't believe in myself. God blessed me when He gave me you as sisters.

To Bethany and Jasmine: thank you for being the proof that I'm not too much or too difficult to love. I've never experienced a sisterhood like the one I have with you, and I am grateful to God that He brought you all into my life.

To Stephanie: having you as an editor was a dream. Thank you for writing my name on that sticky note in your office. Your encouragement has meant the world to me.

To Rachel: you are such a gift to me. Thank you for being the first to believe in this book. You have covered me with encouragement, fought for me, and come alongside me in the most beautiful way.

To Pastor Brandon and Octavia: thank you for pastoring me through the darkest depths of my life.

To my online community: thank you for believing in my words and holding them with grace. Your support fanned the flame of my dream to write a book.

NOTES

Introduction

1. Jackie Pullinger, *Chasing the Dragon: One Woman's Struggle Against the Darkness of Hong Kong's Drug Dens* (London: Hodder & Stoughton, 1980), 58.

2. Jackie Pullinger, *Crack in the Wall: Life & Death in Kowloon Walled City* (London: Hodder & Stoughton, 1993), 15–16.

3. Charles Spurgeon, "Jesus Angry with Hard Hearts," in *Metropolitan Tabernacle Pulpit*, vol. 32 (1886), https://www.spurgeon.org/resource-library/sermons/jesus-angry-with-hard-hearts/#flipbook/.

4. Charles Spurgeon, "The Heart of Flesh: Ezekiel 36:26," in *Metropolitan Tabernacle Pulpit*, vol. 19 (1873), https://www.spurgeon.org/resource-library/sermons/the-heart-of-flesh/#flipbook/.

5. As quoted in Ellen Brown, "Writing Is Third Career for Morrison," *Cincinnati Enquirer* (September 27, 1981), F11.

6. Charles Wesley, "What Sin Hath Done," 1745, https://hymnary.org/text/hearts_of_stone_relent_relent. Public domain.

Chapter 2 Mirages and Mara Moments

1. As quoted in David F. Eisler, *Writing Wars: Authorship and American War Fiction, WW1 to Present* (Iowa City: University of Iowa Press, 2022), xiii.

2. John Mayer, "Slow Dancing in a Burning Room," *Continuum* (Capitol Records, 2006).

3. Joan Didion, "The White Album," in *The White Album: Essays* (New York: Simon & Schuster, 1979), 11.

Chapter 3 Older Brother Syndrome

1. Gwendolyn Brooks, "Paul Robeson," in *The Essential Gwendolyn Brooks* (New York: Library of America, 2005), 176.

Chapter 4 Whales and Weeds

1. *Oxford Advanced Learner's Dictionary*, s.v. "cynicism" (Oxford University Press, 2014), https://www.oxfordlearnersdictionaries.com/us/definition/english/cynicism.

2. C. S. Lewis, *Prince Caspian* (New York: Macmillan, 1970), 130.

3. J. A. Marx, "A Cure for Cynicism," CBN, March 2021, https://www2.cbn.com/devotions/cure-cynicism.

Chapter 5 Forget Thee Not

1. Japp M. J. Murre and Joeri Dros, "Replication and Analysis of Ebbinghaus' Forgetting Curve," *PLoS One* 10, no. 7 (July 2015), doi:10.1371/journal.pone.0120644.

2. Nahum M. Sarna, "Genesis 8:1," *The JPS Torah Commentary: Genesis*, series edited by Nahum M. Sarna and Chaim Potuk (New York: The Jewish Publication Society, 1989), 56.

3. A. W. Tozer, *The Knowledge of the Holy* (New York: HarperOne, 1978), 1.

4. James Weldon Johnson, "O Black and Unknown Bards," in *The Book of American Negro Poetry*, edited by James Weldon Johnson (New York: Harcourt, Brace, 1922). Public domain.

Chapter 6 Joseph's Tears

1. Viola Davis, *Finding Me* (San Francisco: HarperOne, 2022), 6.

2. Davis, *Finding Me*, 6.

3. As quoted in Nancy Thompson, "An Homage to Age and Femininity," *The Flourish Flash Blog*, August 11, 2009, https://flourishpdx.wordpress.com/2009/08/11/an-homage-to-age-and-femininity/.

Chapter 8 The Job Equation

1. Stelman Smith and Judson Cornwall, *The Exhaustive Dictionary of Bible Names* (Alachua, FL: Bridge-Logos, 1998), 64.

2. Alice Walker, *By the Light of My Father's Smile* (New York: Random House, 1998), Kindle loc. 2345.

3. David Guzik, "Job 1—Job Endures His Losses," Enduring Word, accessed July 18, 2023, https://enduringword.com/bible-commentary/job-1/.

Chapter 9 The Melody in the Shipwreck

1. N. T. Wright, *Surprised by Hope: Rethinking Heaven, the Resurrection, and the Mission of the Church* (New York: HarperCollins, 2008), 25.

2. James Strong, *Strong's Expanded Exhaustive Concordance of the Bible*, s.v. "tiqvah" (Nashville: Thomas Nelson, 2009).

3. Emily Dickinson, "'Hope' is the thing with feathers," CommonLit, accessed June 14, 2023, https://www.commonlit.org/en/texts/hope-is -the-thing-with-feathers. Public domain.

Chapter 10 The Gathering of Soft Hearts

1. As quoted in David Guzik, "John 20—An Empty Tomb and a Risen Jesus," Enduring Word, accessed July 18, 2023, https://enduringword.com /bible-commentary/john-20/.

2. Henri J. M. Nouwen, *Life of the Beloved: Spiritual Living in a Secular World* (New York: Crossroad, 1992), 39.

CHARAIA RUSH is a writer and speaker who is passionate about telling the story of the gospel and watching how it softens the hardened corners of our hearts and illuminates the dark rooms of our spirits. She has written for outlets such as *Christian Parenting* and She Reads Truth. She resides in Colorado with her two lovely children.

CONNECT WITH CHARAIA:

CHARAIA.COM

 CharaiaRush